A Constitution for a Democracy

(An excursion in nonfiction)

By Rohit (Roy) Kajaria

ISBN: 9798608896804

For Ma

who left

her footprints

on my life.

The chief foundations of all states, new as well as old or composite, are good laws and good arms;…

Niccolò Machiavelli
In "The Prince", Chapter XII.[1]

They who lay the foundations of a State and furnish it with laws must, as is shown by all who have treated of civil government, and by examples of which history is full, assume that all men are bad, and will always, when they have free field, give loose to their evil inclinations; and that if these for a while remain hidden, it is owing to some secret cause, which, from our having no contrary experience, we do not recognize at once, but which is afterwards revealed by Time, of whom we speak as the father of all truth.

Niccolò Machiavelli
In "Discourses on the first Decade of Titus Livius", Book I, Chapter III.[2]

Since it is necessary, therefore, first to find men, you must come to the Deletto (Draft) of them, as thus the ancients called it, and which we call Scelta (Selection): but in order to call it by a more honored name, I want us to preserve the name of Deletto.

Niccolò Machiavelli
In "The Art of War", Part one.[3]

But it is more necessary than even to regulate property, to take care that the increase of the people should not exceed a certain number; and in determining that, to take into consideration those children who will die, and also those women who will be barren; and to neglect this, as is done in several cities, is to bring certain poverty on the citizens; and poverty is the cause of sedition and evil.

Aristotle in "Politics", Book II, Chapter VI.[4]

It is a general maxim in democracies, oligarchies, monarchies, and indeed in all governments, not to let anyone acquire a rank far superior to the rest of the community, but rather to endeavor to confer moderate honours for a continuance than great ones for a short time; for these latter spoil men, for it is not every one who can bear prosperity:

Aristotle in "Politics", Book V, Chapter VIII.[5]

............therefore it is necessary and most for the benefit of the state that the offices thereof should be filled by the principal persons in it, whose characters are unblemished, and that the people are not oppressed.

Aristotle in "Politics", Book VI, Chapter IV.[6]

But someone may say, that it is wrong to let man have the supreme power and not the law, as his soul is subject to so many passions.

Aristotle in "Politics", Book III, Chapter X.[7]

Contents

Why this book?

Hammurabi, the sixth Amorite king of the first Babylonian dynasty, was born in 1810 B.C., and ruled from 1792 B.C. until his death in 1750 B.C. During his reign, he had expanded his kingdom to cover all of Mesopotamia. He is famous for his code of 282 laws written in Akkadian language on 12 tablets, in 44 columns, and 28 paragraphs. The code was based on the idea of retributive justice or an eye for an eye, and a tooth for a tooth. The code is an early example of a fundamental body of laws ruling a society via a primitive constitution. It is also an early example of the concept of presumption of innocence, the principle that one is considered innocent until proven guilty. The code included both criminal and civil law including civil issues, civil rights, and business contracts. It was promulgated around 1754 B.C. and was put in a public place for all to view. It could be read by any literate person. The purpose was for every citizen to know and understand his or her rights and responsibilities under the law. As the legend goes, Hammurabi received the code from Shamash, the Babylonian god of justice.[8] Things were simpler then.

As the human race advanced, social relationships became more complicated, and as a result laws became more complex. In writing laws, legal jargon replaced the day to day language of a common person, making it difficult for him/her to understand the laws he/she was supposed to obey. Today, it is doubtful that an average citizen in the United States of America (U.S.A. or U.S.) can understand the U.S. Constitution or the laws he/she lives under without the assistance of a lawyer. A government of laws has thus evolved into a government of lawyers. Bills, as proposed laws are called in the U.S. Congress, are so long and complicated that members of Congress do not even have time to read the bills they vote on. Instead, they rely on their staff to read them. Members of Congress then vote on the basis of the input from their staffers. Sometimes lobbyists actually draft a bill, staffers read it, and members of Congress vote on it in order to give the lobbyists what they want. This is the current state of democracy in the U.S. This book, therefore, is an attempt to revert to the simplicity of the code of Hammurabi. A person fluent in English should be able to understand the constitution proposed in this book.

Around 1792,[9] Thomas Jefferson and James Madison created the Democratic-Republican Party to oppose Alexander Hamilton's Federalist Party. However, many framers of the U.S. Constitution did not really appreciate the significance of political parties. As a matter of fact, the word "political parties" does not even appear in the U.S. Constitution. George Washington in his farewell address published in 1796, warned about the dangers of political parties to the government as well as to the country, for he thought that only pragmatists could make this government work, not ideologues. Washington equated political parties with power hungry political ideologues, who would tear the country apart.[10] This was, however, an unrealistic position for Washington to take, given the fact that political parties were as old as the Roman Republic.

James Madison considered a democracy to be the vilest form of government, and Thomas Jefferson equated a democracy to a mob rule. Since "democracy" was a bad word for the founding fathers, the U.S. Constitution was designed to create a republican form of government, not a multi-party democracy. This is reflected in the fact that (a) there was no universal suffrage (until the ratification of the nineteenth amendment),[11] (b) Senators were not elected directly by the people (until the ratification of the seventeenth amendment),[12] but were chosen by the state legislatures,[13] and (c) the President was (and still is) elected by the electoral college (twelfth amendment), and not directly by the people.[14] As a matter of fact, the word "democracy" does not appear anywhere in the U.S. Constitution. The U.S. started out as a republican form of government, and has evolved into what we call a democracy today. The U.S. Constitution establishes three branches of government; a legislative branch consisting of the House of Representatives and the Senate, an executive branch headed by the President, and a judicial branch. For a bill to become a law, it must be voted on favorably by a majority of the House members, a majority of the Senators, and then be signed by the President. If a majority of the House members, a majority of the Senators, and the President belong to the same political party, it is easier to enact a law than if they do not. For example, if a majority of the House members are Democrats, a majority of the Senators are Republicans, and the President is either a Democrat or a Republican, a bill may not be able to move forward, and can get stuck in a stalemate or a political gridlock, if the participants are unwilling to compromise. A constitution, however, should be designed to work with many political parties, since a competition of ideas is healthy for a democracy. Citizens of a republic have different political parties, because they have different world views, which are sometimes irreconcilable.

The U.S. Constitution is written for pragmatists, who want to compromise, not for ideologues who do not. Therefore, the more pragmatists we have in the legislature and in the office of the chief executive, the more functional the legislative process is likely to be. Conversely, the more ideologues we have in these positions, the more dysfunctional it is likely to be.

While some of the inherent shortcomings in the U.S. government today are traceable to the U.S. Constitution, there are also certain advantages. The advantages of a presidential democracy as practiced in accordance with the U.S. Constitution are discussed below:

The first advantage of a presidential democracy is the separation of powers.

The three branches of government are executive, legislative, and judicial. Each branch has its own unique set of authorities and responsibilities. The legislative branch enacts the laws, the executive branch enforces the laws, and the judicial branch interprets the laws. These independent functions provide for checks and balances among the branches of government, limiting the power of each. The branches are constitutionally equal and mutually independent.[15]

The second advantage is stability.

The U.S. has a government regardless of which political party controls the House of Representatives, the Senate or the office of the President. This is not true in a parliamentary democracy like the one in the U.K. In the U.K., a political party or a coalition of political parties with an absolute majority in the House of Commons, can form a government, and elect the Prime Minister as the Chief Executive, from amongst its members. If a political party or a coalition of political parties cannot form an absolute majority in the parliament, there is no government. If a coalition party withdraws from the government, the government may collapse. This is a source of instability in a parliamentary democracy that is absent in a presidential democracy. No political party or a coalition of political parties has to be in a majority in the legislature in order to form a government in the U.S. Also, the Office of the President is extremely stable. As of this writing, Andrew Johnson, William Jefferson (Bill) Clinton, and Donald Trump have been the only three presidents impeached by the House of Representatives, but none of them were convicted by the Senate.

Some of the shortcomings of the government framework specified in the U.S. Constitution are as follows:

The first shortcoming is a built-in potential for a political stalemate or a gridlock.

Unless the two legislative houses and the President belong to the same political party, a political stalemate or a gridlock is a real possibility. Also, having a bicameral legislature or two legislative houses, such as a Senate and a House of Representatives, increases the likelihood of a gridlock, if different political parties are in a majority in each legislative house. A parliamentary democracy, like the one in the United Kingdom (U.K.), also has two houses: the House of Commons and the House of Lords. However, the House of Lords, which is the upper house, has limited powers. For example, the power of the House of Lords to reject a bill passed by the House of Commons is severely restricted by the Parliament Acts. Under these Acts, for certain types of bills, the House of Commons can override the veto by the House of Lords. The House of Lords cannot delay a money bill for more than one month. A money bill or a supply bill is a bill that solely concerns taxation or government spending (also known as appropriation of money), as opposed to changes in public law.[16]

Other public bills cannot be delayed by the House of Lords for more than two parliamentary sessions, or one calendar year. The House of Lords may neither originate a bill concerning taxation or supply of treasury or exchequer funds, nor amend a bill so as to insert a taxation or supply-related provision. Moreover, the Upper House may not amend any supply bill.[17] This, however, is not the case with the U.S. Senate.

While a separation of powers is functional, a gridlock is political. The President, the House of Representatives or the Senate leadership can shut down the government, if they want to, by not enacting legislation to fund the government. A constitution should be written with provisions that provide for the continuity of government funding regardless of the political parties in control of the legislative bodies and the office of the chief executive. While the strength of a presidential democracy is its stability, its weakness is the very real potential for political gridlock. This situation also undermines accountability. Two political parties can always blame each other for the gridlock, with neither held accountable. The constitution proposed in this book addresses this by incorporating some of the elements of a parliamentary democracy, and by establishing only one legislative chamber or a unicameral legislature at the federal, state, and city levels.

The second shortcoming of the U.S. Constitution is that the eligibility criteria for a person to hold the office of the President are minimal.

As specified in Article II, Section 1.5 of the U.S. Constitution, the only criteria are that one be at least 35 years old, a natural born Citizen, and a resident of the U.S. for no less than fourteen years.[18]

Similarly, Article I, Section 2.2 specifies the eligibility criteria to be a Representative as no less than twenty five years of age and be a Citizen of the U.S. for no less than seven years.[19] Article I, Section 3.3 specifies the eligibility criteria to be a Senator as no less than thirty years of age and be a Citizen of the U.S. for no less than nine years.[20] The eligibility criterion to hold the Office of a Judge is good behavior, i.e. for life.[21]

One of the few things that provides a likely indicator of success in human affairs is relevant experience. In most of the professions, people are hired on the basis of their qualifications and experience. This is not true of the U.S. political system. Any thirty-five-year-old natural born U.S. citizen can run for the President, independently of his/her qualifications or political experience. Being thirty-five years old is a chronological fact, not a qualification to become the President of the United States. However, in the U.S., an unqualified candidate with no political experience can run and be elected president, since the qualification requirements are minimal. The U.S. political system rewards performance on the campaign trail, which has little to do with a person's ability to govern. Political governance is a professional field, and as in any other field, experience and qualifications do matter. Empirical knowledge does matter. Temperament does matter. Experience may not always tell one what to do, but it may tell one what not to do. In politics as in real life, where many major decisions are made under the conditions of uncertainty, this is important. One would like to live under a good leader, but what is the constitutional mechanism to provide qualified and experienced leaders? The quality and quantity of experience, therefore, can be considered a valid criterion to elect a good leader. Given a certain continuity in human nature, a person is likely to continue behaving in the same way as he/she did in the past. In other words, an industrious person is likely to continue being industrious, and a lazy person is likely to continue being lazy. This book sets rigorous age, qualification and experience criteria for the position of the President and also for other public offices. Also, this book replaces the ambiguous term "natural born" with the more specific term "born in the republic". [22]

The third shortcoming of the U.S. constitution is that the number of justices in the Supreme Court is not specified.

Article III of the U.S. Constitution leaves this matter to the Congress. The Federal Judiciary Act of 1789 created the U.S. Supreme Court and Federal District Courts. This act called for a Chief Justice and five associate justices, for a total of six justices in the U.S. Supreme Court. This number was increased to seven in 1807, to nine in 1837, and to ten in 1863. The Judicial Circuits Act of 1866 reduced the number of justices from ten to seven. The decrease was to take place by attrition. However, in 1869 there were still eight justices. The judiciary act of 1869 added one more justice to make it nine. This number has not changed since.[23] However, the Judicial Procedures Reform Bill of 1937 (frequently called the "court-packing plan") was a legislative initiative proposed by the U.S. President Franklin D. Roosevelt to add more justices to the U.S. Supreme Court. Roosevelt's intent was to obtain favorable rulings regarding New Deal legislation that the court had ruled unconstitutional. The central provision of the bill would have granted the President power to appoint an additional Justice to the U.S. Supreme Court, up to a maximum of six, for every member of the court over the age of 70 years and 6 months.[24] Thus, it is necessary to specify the number of judges in every court, in order to limit the politicization of the judiciary. Additionally, there are no official qualifications specified for Supreme Court Justices. This is an important detail that is missing, and needs to be provided in a constitution, as the proposed constitution in this book does.

The fourth shortcoming is that the ability of the Supreme Court to declare a legislative or an executive act unconstitutional based on a judicial review is not specified in the U.S. Constitution.

The U.S. Supreme Court under Chief Justice John Marshall established this doctrine in the case of Marbury v. Madison (1803).[25] This is an important judicial function that is missing from the U.S. Constitution.

The fifth shortcoming is that no age limit is specified for the mandatory retirement of a government employee.

The U.S. Constitution does not specify any mandatory age limit for retiring a government employee. As people age, their health tends to decline, as evidenced by the spending on health care. Also, the likelihood of cognitive impairment increases. In the U.S., the average personal health care spending for the 65 and older population was over 5 times higher than spending per child and approximately 3 times the spending per working-age person. The elderly were nearly 14 percent of the population, and accounted for approximately 34 percent of all health care spending in 2012.[26] If health care spending is an indicator of health, the health of an average person declines after the age of sixty-five. Also, the prevalence of Mild Cognitive Impairment (MCI) increases with age. (The prevalence of MCI among different age groups is as follows: 6.7% for ages 60–64, 8.4% for ages 65–69, 10.1% for ages 70–74, 14.8% for ages 75–79, and 25.2% for ages 80–84. After a two-year follow-up, the cumulative incidence of dementia among individuals who are over 65 years old and were diagnosed with MCI was found to be 14.9%.) Globally, approximately 16% of the population over the age of 70 experiences some type of MCI (or incipient dementia).[27] More importantly, no matter how great an individual may be, the republic is always greater. A good republic should have room for individual initiative and ambition. However, the health and interests of the republic are always more important than those of an individual. Therefore, seventy is a reasonable mandatory retirement age for every elected and unelected government employee, as specified in this book.[28]

The sixth shortcoming is that important concepts are not defined in the U.S. Constitution.

The U.S. Constitution and other constitutions that the author has reviewed, do not define the important concepts used, such as, liberty, equality, and justice. Since a concept can mean different things to different people, the important concepts used in a constitution need to be defined as they apply to that constitution. This book defines important concepts used in the book in terms of their intended meanings.

The seventh shortcoming is that there is no provision to overturn even a split Supreme Court decision.

A split decision is the one that is not unanimous. The U.S. system of government is based on checks and balances among the executive, legislative and the judicial branches. However, the U.S. Supreme Court is the ultimate, unchallenged authority on the interpretation of the U.S. Constitution. Even when the decision is split and controversial (e.g. Citizens United v. Federal Election Commission, 558 U.S. 310 (2010)),[29] there is no way to overturn it, except through a constitutional amendment. This is very difficult, expensive, and therefore, impractical. This book specifies a legislative method to provide this critical check and balance to the judiciary.

The eighth shortcoming is that the official language of the republic is not specified in the U.S. constitution.

The French constitution in Title I, Article 2 specifies French to be the language of the republic.[30] The U.S. Constitution does not identify the official language of the republic. It is important to specify the official language, so that every legal resident of the republic reads, writes, and speaks this language fluently. This facilitates efficient communication and standardization. A language is a unifying force, which provides a sense of belonging in a country. Having a common language is also efficient and cost effective, since the government does not have to spend time and money on translating and publishing the same information in multiple languages.

The ninth shortcoming is that tough political decisions which are unpopular, but vital to the health of the republic, such as, a requirement to balance the budget or a requirement for a military draft are not specified.

Since democracies are not good at enacting tough requirements, a constitution should not leave these requirements to politicians, who can politicize them. Politicians in a democracy want to be popular, so they can get elected and reelected. Voting on an unpopular requirement, such as, increasing taxes or cutting the government spending in order to balance the budget does not make politicians popular, and does not help them politically. However, a constitution that is difficult to amend can provide a good excuse for forcing the right decision. If unpopular requirements are specified in the constitution, politicians have no choice but to abide by them. For example, the German and the Russian Constitutions specify the military draft.[31]

The tenth shortcoming is that Article I, Section 5.2 of the U.S Constitution allows each house of the U.S. Congress to determine the rules of its proceedings without any constraints.[32]

This in turn, has allowed the U.S. Senate to create a cloture rule to end the filibuster that violates the majority rule of a democracy. A cloture is a motion or process in parliamentary procedure aimed at bringing debate to a quick end.[33] A filibuster is a political procedure where one or more members of parliament or congress debate over a proposed piece of legislation so as to delay or entirely prevent a decision being made on the proposal.[34] A filibuster is a dilatory or obstructive tactic used in the United States Senate to prevent a measure from being brought to a vote.

The most common form of filibuster occurs when one or more senators attempt to delay or block a vote on a bill by extending debate on the measure. The Senate rules permit a senator, or a series of senators, to speak for as long as they wish, and on any topic they choose, unless "three-fifths of the Senators duly chosen and sworn" (usually 60 out of 100) bring the debate to a close by invoking cloture under Senate Rule XXII.[35] Thus, today, one needs sixty percent majority vote in the Senate in order to avoid a filibuster, and vote on a bill. This means that a minority of forty-one senators can impose its will on the majority of fifty-nine senators as in an oligarchy, rather than a majority imposing its will on the minority as in a democracy. The U.S. constitution allows this, and it needs to be fixed. The proposed constitution in this book requires a legislative chamber to abide by the majority rule of a democracy in making its rules.

The eleventh shortcoming is that the U.S. Constitution does not provide for the direct election of the President by the citizens, but instead has created an opaque entity called the Electoral College.

It is a common misunderstanding that U.S. voters directly elect their Presidents. They do not. The U.S. Constitution gives states, not individual citizens, a right to vote for and elect the President. As George Mason, a delegate from Virginia to the constitutional convention in Philadelphia in 1787, said, "it were as unnatural to refer the choice of a proper character for Chief Magistrate to the people, as it would be to refer a trial of colors to a blind man."[36] Thus the founding fathers of the U.S. did not want a direct election of the President. When U.S. citizens vote for a Presidential candidate, they are actually voting for their candidate's electors in their respective states. The candidates running for a general Presidential election in a state have their own group of electors in the state. The Electoral College consists of 538 electors. There is one elector per house member, one elector per U.S. Senator, and three electors allocated to the District of Columbia. An absolute majority of 270 electoral votes is required to elect the President. The individual electors are generally chosen by the Presidential candidate's political party sometime before the general election. In most states, the political parties nominate the slate of electors at state conventions or at central committee meetings. On election day, the voters in each state elect their state's electors by casting their ballots for the President. This happens every four years during the Presidential election year on the Tuesday after the first Monday in November (e.g. on 8 November 2016). The electors meet in their respective states on the Monday after the second Wednesday in December after the Presidential election (e.g. on 19 December 2016), to cast their votes for the President and the Vice-President in separate ballots.[37] The Electoral College is not a process transparent to an average U.S. citizen. It is a vestige of the Republican form of government our Founding Fathers designed and built, which, unlike a democracy, was not meant for a common citizen. There is no Constitutional provision that requires Electors to vote according to the results of the popular vote in their states. The winner is elected by an absolute majority of the electoral votes rather than by a simple majority of the popular vote. In a parliamentary democracy, the Prime Minister, who is the Head of Government, is also elected indirectly by an absolute majority vote of the members of parliament rather than by a popular vote. However, unlike the Electoral College, the members of parliament are elected directly by the people in a popular vote. Article II, Section 1, Amendment XII, and Amendment XXIII, Section 1 of the constitution specify the rules for electing a President.[38] However, the language needs to be simpler for a citizen to understand, without help of a lawyer. Since the Electoral College is required by the U.S. constitution, replacing it with a direct election (or a different procedure) would take a constitutional amendment. This is very difficult, expensive, time consuming, and therefore, impractical. The approach taken in this book makes the Electoral College unnecessary.

The twelfth shortcoming is that a constitutional convention is not well defined. Article V of the U.S. Constitution specifies a constitutional convention as a means of amending the constitution.[39]

However, the details regarding a constitutional convention are not well defined. For example, who are the members of this convention, how are they selected, how many members are there, what is the scope of the convention in terms of what can be discussed, what are the boundaries in terms of time limit, what are the controls on the convention, and who exercises them. Can the convention repeal the thirteenth amendment abolishing slavery or the nineteenth amendment giving women a right to vote, or any of the other amendments? This is not clear. Since detailed procedures are necessary to make a convention work, these procedures need to be specified. The proposed constitution in this book eliminates the constitutional convention as a method of amending the constitution.

The thirteenth shortcoming is that the U.S. Constitution covers only the federal government.

The purpose of a constitution is to specify the structure and processes of the government. Article IV, Section 4 of the U.S. Constitution guarantees every state in the U.S. a Republican Form of Government.[40] However, it does not provide any details as to how to set up this government. Consequently, each state in the U.S. has its own constitution and its own body of constitutional law. This creates a non-uniform constitutional and legal system in the country, which is complex, anachronistic and inefficient. The proposed constitution in this book covers the federal, state and city governments in a fair amount of detail with efficiency and standardization in mind.

The fourteenth shortcoming is that the seventh amendment to the U.S. Constitution allows the right to a trial by jury in a federal civil trial, if the value in controversy exceeds twenty dollars.[41]

Twenty dollars may have been a significant amount when this amendment was drafted, but it is an insignificant amount today due to inflation. For this reason, a fixed dollar amount should not be specified in a constitution.

The fifteenth shortcoming is that Article II, Section 2.1 of the U.S. Constitution gives the President power to grant Reprieves and Pardons for Offences against the United States, except in Cases of Impeachment.[42]

This violates the fundamental principle of separation of powers on which the U.S. government is based by giving the judicial authority to the executive. Once the judiciary finds a person guilty after an elaborate judicial process, it is not clear as to what more evidence the President would have to reverse that decision.

Additionally, as George Mason in the anti-Federalist paper, "Objections to This Constitution of Government" wrote in 1787: "The President of the United States has the unrestrained power of granting pardons for treason; which may be sometimes exercised to screen from punishment those whom he had secretly instigated to commit the crime, and thereby prevent a discovery of his own guilt." Thus, a President can obstruct justice through his/her power to grant Reprieves and Pardons.

Therefore, the proposed constitution in this book does not give an executive power to grant reprieves and pardons for offences.

The sixteenth shortcoming is that Article III, Section 2.3 of the U.S. Constitution requires a trial by jury in all criminal trials.[43]

In addition to infringing upon the freedom of private citizens who are required to serve as jurors, the entire process is inefficient with no evidence of a fairer outcome. A jury made up of ordinary citizens with no legal background is much more susceptible to emotional manipulation by prosecution and defense lawyers than judges who themselves are lawyers. As Mark Twain wrote in his book "Roughing It" in 1880: "The jury system puts a ban upon intelligence and honesty, and a premium upon ignorance, stupidity and perjury. It is a shame that we must continue to use a worthless system because it was good a thousand years ago."[44] Therefore, the proposed constitution in this book does not allow for a trial by jury.

The United Kingdom (U.K.) provides another example of a democracy. The government of the U.K. is based on a parliamentary model formed in 1707, which is unlike the presidential model specified in the U.S. constitution that was drafted in 1787, ratified in 1788, and became official in 1789.[45] While the British constitution is not codified, the processes of the British government are well established by centuries of tradition. Some advantages and shortcomings of the British parliamentary democracy are described in the following paragraphs.

Advantages of the British parliamentary form of democracy are:

The first advantage of the U.K. parliamentary form of democracy is that there is greater accountability.

Since a political party or a coalition of political parties that is in the absolute majority in the legislature makes up the government, and is responsible for passing all the legislation, it cannot blame the opposition parties for lack of results. This blame game is common in a presidential democracy. Also, since the executive and the legislative functions are part of the same body, the relationship between the two functions is not as adversarial as in a Presidential democracy.

The second advantage of the U.K. parliamentary model is that there is greater legislative efficiency.

Since the government is usually (except in a coalition government) made up of the political party with an absolute majority in the legislature (majority government),[46] the legislative process is more efficient than in a presidential democracy. When no single political party has an absolute majority in a legislature, the parliament is hung.[47] When no single political party has an absolute majority in a legislature, it tries to form an alliance with other political parties until the coalition of parties reaches an absolute majority necessary to form a government. This is called a coalition government.[48] The political party or parties that are in a minority form the opposition to the government.

The third advantage is that the U.K. parliamentary form of government is more cost effective.

Since the House of Commons in the parliament (the federal legislature) elects the chief executive of government (the prime minister), and the people elect the House of Commons, the election cycle is much shorter, and therefore, more cost effective than in a presidential democracy. As a result, there is no country wide ticket as in the U.S. presidential democracy. Since there are no primaries, candidates chosen by their political parties run for seats in federal legislative districts. The winners become members of the House of Commons (or members of parliament), and elect the chief executive of the government or the Prime Minister.

With every election cycle, the U.S. is spending more and more money to elect its public officials, with no better results in terms of the quality of leadership. This means that the U.S. democracy is becoming less and less cost-effective.

Also, the U.S. election campaigns are much longer compared to the parliamentary democracies such as, Canada and the U.K., and seem to last forever. The money for the ever more expensive campaigns increasingly comes from wealthy people and corporations, making this more and more of a government by the wealthy or a plutocracy, and less and less of a democracy. The U.S. Constitution as written, has no way to prevent this. The constitution proposed in this book addresses these issues.

The fourth advantage is that there is no direct election of the Prime Minister, who is the chief executive of the government in the U.K.

The Prime Minister is elected by an absolute majority vote of the House of Commons in the Parliament (the federal legislature), rather than by the people through the Electoral College as in the U.S. While a multitude of common citizens is less susceptible to corruption than legislators, it is more susceptible to emotional manipulation by the politicians and the media than are the legislators, who elect the chief executive. Politicians judge other politicians with a different set of criteria than average citizens do. In a parliamentary democracy, one who wants to be a chief executive, not only has to win his/her own election, but has to take his/her party to a victory in order to achieve an absolute majority necessary to form the government (except in a coalition government). This requires a different set of qualities in terms of knowledge and experience, as compared to winning one's own seat in an election as in a presidential democracy.

Some of the shortcomings of the British parliamentary form of democracy are identified in the following paragraphs:

The first shortcoming is the instability caused by breakdown of a coalition government.

In order to form a Government, a political party must be able to command a majority in the House of Commons on votes of confidence and supply. A confidence-and supply agreement is one whereby a party or independent members of parliament will support the government in motions of confidence and appropriation or budget (supply) votes.[49] This majority can include support from other political parties, whether or not there is a formal coalition arrangement.

When a general election results in no single political party winning an overall majority in the House of Commons, this is known as a situation of no overall control, or a 'hung Parliament'. If the incumbent government is unable to command a majority and decides to resign, the leader of the largest opposition party may be invited to form a government and may do so either as a minority or in coalition with another party or parties.

The Prime Minister only has to resign, if it is clear that he/she cannot command a majority of the House of Commons on votes of confidence or supply. This would be the case if the incumbent government fails to make a deal with one or more of the other political parties, or if they lose a confidence motion in the House of Commons.[50] If one or more coalition partners withdraw from the government, and if the government loses the absolute majority in the legislature, it falls apart, thus leading to instability. The proposed constitution in this book attempts to solve this problem by injecting elements of the presidential democracy into a primarily parliamentary democracy government model.

The second shortcoming is that there is no separation of powers between the executive and the legislative functions.

Since it is the legislature that elects the chief executive of the government, he/she is part of the legislature, and not an independent entity. This makes him/her dependent on the legislature to keep his/her job. However, this is a trade-off that provides legislative efficiency. As a result, the political gridlock in the U.S. democracy that is described earlier, is avoided.

The third shortcoming is that the legislation passed by the British parliament is not subject to a judicial review.

Since parliamentary sovereignty is a principle of the U.K. constitution, the laws passed by the British parliament are not subject to a judicial review for their constitutionality as they are in the U.S. This makes Parliament the supreme legal and constitutional authority in the U.K., which can create or end any law. Generally, the courts cannot overrule parliamentary legislation.[51] In the U.K., a judicial review is a type of court proceeding in which a judge reviews the lawfulness of a decision or action made by a public body. It is not really concerned with the conclusions of that process and whether those were 'right', as long as the right procedures have been followed. The court will not substitute what it thinks is the 'correct' decision.[52]

In absence of a judicial check on the legislative function, and thereby, the executive function, the parliament and the executive can become very powerful. The proposed constitution in this book incorporates a check that allows the judiciary to interpret the constitution and determine the constitutionality of an executive or a legislative act.

The fourth shortcoming is that the U.K. constitution allows a Prime Minister to suspend the parliament.

This provision, no matter how well meaning, allows a Prime Minister to suspend the parliament for political reasons. This undermines the British democracy, and therefore, is a shortcoming. The proposed constitution in this book does not allow an executive to suspend the legislature.

The fifth shortcoming is that the U.K. constitution allows the unelected members of a political party to directly elect the Prime Minister.

A prime minister belongs to the entire country, not just to a political party. Therefore, he/she should be elected by the elected members of the parliament, not by the unelected members of a political party. The proposed constitution in this book requires the elected legislators to elect the executive.

The sixth shortcoming is that the sovereignty of the parliament makes the Prime Minister subservient to the parliament rather than its co-equal.

Since the Prime Minister cannot veto a bill passed by the majority of the parliament, it becomes a law, whether the Prime Minister agrees with it or not. This means that the Prime Minister has to comply with and implement the law he/she may not agree with. Any non-compliance with the law means that the Prime Minister is in contempt of court, and can be sent to prison. The proposed constitution in this book allows an executive to veto a bill passed by an absolute majority vote of the legislature. A vetoed bill, however, can be overridden by a super majority vote of the legislature.

Nothing in this proposed constitution is cast in concrete. It is to be tailored to the individual needs of a country, based on variables such as, its history, geography, culture, language, size, population, and religion, among others. This proposed constitution, therefore, is a starting point, not an end point. The book is written for general use, and can be used by any country interested in a secular democracy as a form of government. Like any human endeavor, it is imperfect, and can always be improved upon.

In the final analysis, the purpose of this book is to add value to the world we live in, and to make a difference. Aristotle, during his life, could not find a constitution that was entirely satisfactory.[53] This book is an attempt to address that concern, which is still valid. I am not a lawyer by profession, but then neither was Hammurabi. Probably 34 out of 55 members of the U.S. Constitutional Convention held in Philadelphia in 1787 had at least made a study of the law. In addition to the lawyers, soldiers, planters, educators, ministers, physicians, financiers, and merchants were members of the U.S. Constitutional Convention.[54] George Washington, who presided over the 1787 convention that drafted the United States Constitution, did not attend college.[55] James Madison, the father of the U.S. Constitution, was not trained as a lawyer.[56] That is my excuse and my consolation for writing this book. Happy reading.

- RK

The Proposed Constitution

The purpose of a constitution is to design the structure and processes of a government. A constitution should be designed in such a manner that it leads to an efficient, cost-effective, accountable, and a stable democracy independently of the political ideologies, pragmatism or temperament of the constituent members of the government.   The constitution proposed in this book is an attempt in that direction.

Two basic models of democracy in the world today are the parliamentary form of democracy as practiced in the U.K. since 1707, and the presidential form of democracy as practiced in the U.S. since 1789. The proposed constitution in this book is primarily based on the parliamentary model of democracy as practiced in the U.K. (with some elements of the presidential form of democracy as practiced in the U.S.). This form of government is legislatively more efficient, more cost-effective, and provides greater accountability. While it may result in political instability because of coalition governments, this issue is easier to solve than the problem of a stalemate or a political gridlock inherent in the U.S. Presidential democracy. In the proposed constitution, it takes a simple rather than an absolute majority vote of the legislature to elect the executives, and to approve the cabinet members and the judges. This makes it easier to form the government. However, it takes a super rather than an absolute majority vote of the legislature to remove them. Thus, the executives are elected for a five-year term, and a vote of no-confidence to dismantle the government takes a super majority vote of the legislature. This makes the government more difficult to dismantle, and therefore, more stable than the parliamentary democracy as practiced in the U.K. In general, a stable government is more likely to be effective than an unstable one. To solve the problem of political stalemate or gridlock, structurally, one needs a unicameral legislature, which improves the legislative efficiency; politically, one needs the same political party in control of the legislative and the executive branches of government; and behaviorally, one needs pragmatic politicians who want to compromise. These conditions are difficult, if not impossible to meet in a Presidential democracy as practiced in the U.S.

Some of the significant aspects of the government defined in this proposed constitution are as follows: the government has three functions: executive, legislative and judicial. The executive enforces the laws, the legislature makes the laws, and the judiciary interprets the laws. Only a citizen born in the republic is eligible for an election to or an appointment to a public office. The mandatory retirement age for every government employee is seventy years.

Any citizen of the republic, who meets the eligibility criteria specified in this proposed constitution, can run for an election to a public office, and can reach the top of the political mountain, provided he/she starts at the bottom, and climbs all the way to the top overcoming all the obstacles encountered. It does not matter, whether he/she climbs the mountain from left, right, or center, as long as he/she climbs the entire mountain. This ensures that the candidate has the necessary qualifications and experience for the top job, and that he/she has paid his/her dues to reach the top.

In the interest of simplicity and efficiency, the legislature in the proposed constitution is unicameral. This means that there is only one legislative chamber at each level of government; the Senate at the federal level, the Congress at the state level, and the City Council (or simply the Council) at the city level. Each Senator, Congressperson, and City Councilperson has one vote in the respective legislative chamber.

A Senator is elected for five years by the eligible voters of a Senate district. A Congressperson is elected for five years by the eligible voters of a Congressional district. A City Councilperson is elected for five years by the eligible voters of a City Council district. Each legislature elects a Speaker for the legislative term by a simple majority vote.

The minimum age requirement for a Congressperson or a Councilperson to serve is twenty-five years. The minimum age requirement for a Senator to serve is thirty-five years.

The number of Senators allocated to a state are directly proportional to the number of citizens in the state. The average number of senators per state is ten. No state has less than one Senator. Each Senator represents roughly the same number of citizens. The number of Congresspersons in a state is directly proportional to the number of citizens in the state. The least populated state has twenty-five and the most populated state has one hundred Congresspersons. Each Congressperson represents roughly the same number of citizens. The number of City Councilpersons in a city are directly proportional to the number of citizens in the city. The least populated city has twenty-five and the most populated city has fifty City Councilpersons. Each City Councilperson represents roughly the same number of citizens.

To remove a Senator requires a super majority vote in the Senate. To remove a Congressperson requires a super majority vote in the Congress of that state. To remove a Councilperson requires a super majority vote in the City Council of that city.

The President is the chief executive of the federal government. He/she is also the commander in chief of the armed forces and the head of state. The President and the Vice-President of the republic are elected as a pair by the Senate for a period of five years with a simple majority vote. They are incumbent Senators from the same political party, and continue to perform their duties as Senators. A Governor is the chief executive of a state. The Governor and the Deputy Governor are elected as a pair by the Congress of the state for a period of five years with a simple majority vote. They are incumbent Congresspersons from the same political party, and continue to perform their duties as

Congresspersons. A Mayor is the chief executive of a city. The Mayor and the Deputy Mayor of a city are elected as a pair by the City Council for a period of five years with a simple majority vote. They are incumbent City Councilpersons from the same political party, and continue to perform their duties as City Councilpersons.

The minimum age requirement for a President or a Vice-President to serve is fifty years. The minimum age requirement for a Governor or a Deputy Governor to serve is thirty-five years. The minimum age requirement for a Mayor or a Deputy Mayor to serve is thirty years. No person can be elected as a President, a Vice-President, a Governor, a Deputy Governor, a Mayor, or a Deputy Mayor for more than two five-year terms before the mandatory retirement age of seventy years for government employees.

To remove a President or a Vice-President requires a super majority vote in the Senate. To remove a Governor or a Deputy Governor requires a super majority vote in the Congress of that state. To remove a Mayor or a Deputy Mayor requires a super majority vote in the City Council of that city.

No more than one vote of no confidence is allowed at any level of government in a period of five years.

A vote of no confidence in the federal government requires a super majority vote in the Senate. Once the Senate passes the vote of no confidence, the President, the Vice-President, and all the Cabinet Secretaries have to resign their positions in the government. They can still retain their jobs as Senators. A new President and a new Vice-President from the same political party are elected as a pair by a simple majority vote of the Senate. Any Senator eligible to become a President or a Vice-President is allowed to run for these offices. If no pair gets a simple majority vote in the Senate, there is a run-off election between the top two pairs. The pair that gets the simple majority vote in the Senate, becomes the new President and the new Vice-President. The new President selects the new Cabinet Secretaries, who, once confirmed by a simple majority vote of the Senate, form the new government.

A vote of no confidence in the state government requires a super majority vote in the Congress of that state. Once the Congress passes the vote of no confidence, the Governor, the Deputy Governor, and all the Cabinet Secretaries have to resign their positions in the government. They can still retain their jobs as Congresspersons. A new Governor and a new Deputy Governor from the same political party are elected as a pair by a simple majority vote of the Congress. Any Congressperson eligible to become a Governor or a Deputy Governor is allowed to run for these offices. If no pair gets a simple majority vote in the Congress, there is a run-off election between the top two pairs. The pair that gets the simple majority vote in the Congress, becomes the new Governor and the new Deputy Governor. The new Governor selects the new Cabinet Secretaries, who, once confirmed by a simple majority vote of the Congress, form the new government.

A vote of no confidence in the city government requires a super majority vote in the City Council of that city. Once the City Council passes the vote of no confidence, the Mayor, the Deputy Mayor, and all the Cabinet Secretaries have to resign their positions in the government. They can still retain their jobs as Councilpersons. A new Mayor and a new Deputy Mayor from the same political party are elected as a pair by a simple majority vote of the City Council. Any Councilperson eligible to become a Mayor or a Deputy Mayor is allowed to run for these offices. If no pair gets a simple majority vote in the City Council, there is a run-off election between the top two pairs. The pair that gets the simple majority vote in the City Council, becomes the new Mayor and the new Deputy Mayor. The new Mayor selects the new Cabinet Secretaries, who, once confirmed by a simple majority vote of the City Council, form the new government

The judiciary is divided into the District Court, the Appeals Court, and the Supreme Court in an ascending order of priority at the federal and the state level. A judicial decision, in general, is primarily based on a statute, and secondarily on a legal precedent or a norm or a custom, if no statute is available. The judges are the main investigators. The legal system is inquisitorial rather than adversarial. District Courts decide cases on the basis of facts and the law. Appeals Courts decide cases only on the basis of law. An appeals process is an examination of specific errors made by the lower court.

The federal court judges are appointed by the President and are confirmed by a simple majority vote of the Senate. The state court judges are appointed by the Governor of the state and are confirmed by a simple majority vote of the Congress of that state. To remove a federal judge from the bench requires a super majority vote in the Senate. To remove a state judge from the bench requires a super majority vote in the Congress of that state.

The minimum age requirement for a District Court judge to serve is thirty years. The minimum age requirement for an Appeals court judge to serve is forty years. The minimum age requirement for a Supreme Court judge to serve is fifty years.

Each court has three judges. The chief judge in each court is the most senior judge. The chief judge of the federal Supreme Court is the head of the federal judiciary, and is called the chief justice of the republic. The chief judge of the state Supreme Court is the head of the state judiciary, and is called the chief justice of the state.

The judicial process is in the following order: (a). the state District Court, the state Appeals Court in the same state, the state Supreme Court in the same state, the federal Supreme Court, and the Senate or (b). the federal District Court, the federal Appeals Court in the same state, the federal Supreme Court, and the Senate.

There is no trial by jury. A unanimous decision by a court is considered final. A split decision by a court may be appealed to a higher court. Like the U.S. and unlike the U.K., there is judicial oversight of the constitutionality of legislative and executive acts. However, unlike the U.S. and the U.K., the check on the judiciary is provided by the super majority vote of the Senate to overturn the decision of the federal Supreme Court. But for the judges of the federal Supreme Court, every judge is transferred randomly to an equivalent position every ten years.

A Constitution for a Democracy

Preamble: We, the people of this republic, in order to provide freedom and justice for all, law and order to ensure domestic peace, strong defense against external threat, a good life for citizens by promoting the common good, and establish a stable, transparent, accountable, efficient, and cost-effective democratic government, promulgate this constitution. We maintain that justice requires equality before the law, even though no two individuals are created exactly alike in every respect. This constitution is the supreme law of the land. What is not in this constitution may be established by laws compatible with the constitution.[57]

Chapter I: General Provisions

Article 1 The Language.

English shall be the official language of the republic.[58]

Article 2 The Republic and the Flag.

2.1 The republic shall be a democracy for the people, by the people, and of the people, one nation united under the flag and this constitution.[59]

2.2 The motto of the republic shall be liberty, equality, and secularity.[60]

2.3 The national flag shall not be desecrated, and shall be the only flag displayed on the grounds of a public property.

2.4 Upon death of a prominent citizen, the national flag shall be flown at half-staff on the grounds of a public property as follows: a. six days throughout the republic for the President and the Vice-President; b. five days in the national capital for Senators and Federal Judges; c. four days throughout the state for Governors and Deputy Governors; d. three days in the state capital for Congresspersons and State Judges; e. two days in the city for Mayors and Deputy Mayors; f. one day in the city for City Councilpersons; g. three days in the national capital for prominent citizens outside the government, as designated by a super majority vote of the Senate.

2.5 Upon death of the President or the Vice-President, there shall be a state funeral and a day of national mourning. Upon death of a prominent citizen, there shall be a state funeral and a day of national mourning, if approved by a super majority vote of the Senate.

2.6 No part of the republic shall be considered sovereign, autonomous or independent of the republic.

2.7 Legal residents of the republic shall enjoy the rights specified in this constitution with an understanding that rights imply responsibilities.

Article 3 The Supreme Law and Precedence.

3.1 This constitution and the laws derived from it shall be sovereign in the republic.[61] There shall be no other constitution in the republic.

3.2 This constitution shall be the foundation of all federal, state, and local laws.[62]

3.3 All the discrepancies in the laws shall be resolved in the following order of precedence: this constitution, federal laws, international treaties of the republic, state laws and local laws.[63] No local or state law contradicting a federal law shall be enacted, unless a waiver has been granted by a super majority vote of the Senate subsequent to a petition from the applicable city Mayor or the state Governor respectively. No local law contradicting the state law shall be enacted, unless a waiver has been granted by a super majority vote of the state Congress subsequent to a petition from the applicable city Mayor.

3.4 All the discrepancies in judicial decisions shall be resolved in the following order of precedence: federal Supreme Court, federal appeals court, federal district court, state Supreme Court, state appeals court, and state district court.

Article 4 Secularity.

4.1 The republic shall have no official religion or ideology.[64]

4.2 The secularity of the republic shall not be undermined.

4.3 The government shall respect every religion equally.

4.4 Religious practice being a private matter, no religion shall be allowed in a public institution.

4.5 No religion shall interfere with a government function.

4.6 The government shall not interfere with a religion, unless it violates a law.

4.7 No political party shall have a religious or a military dimension.

4.8 No religion shall have a political or a military dimension.

4.9 The military shall not have a religious or a political dimension.

Article 5 Equality.

5.1 Every person and entity with a legal status in the republic, shall be treated equally in the court of law.[65]

5.2 No one shall be above or beneath the law.

5.3 No legislature shall exempt itself from the laws it enacts for the general public.

5.4 Equality of rights under the law shall not be denied, or otherwise abridged on account of race, sex, sexual orientation, religion, caste, tribe or national origin of a legal resident.

5.5 No legal resident shall be identified by his/her race, religion, caste, nationality or tribe.

Article 6 Freedom.

6.1 Citizens shall be guaranteed a right to the pluralistic expression of opinions and to the equitable participation in the democratic life of the republic.[66]

6.2 Freedom of speech, freedom of the press, the right of people to assemble peacefully and to petition their elected representatives and judiciary for grievances shall not be abridged, except for falsehoods that undermine reputation and words that undermine public safety or national security or are obscene.[67]

6.3 A legal resident shall have freedom to travel except as constrained by law.[68]

6.4 Legal residents shall have access to government records upon request as long as the public interest or the national security is not undermined.

6.5 Legal residents shall have a right to privacy except as constrained by law.

Article 7 Right to vote.

7.1 Every citizen, eighteen years of age or older, shall have a right to cast one vote for each public office in an election, a referendum, and an initiative. This right of universal suffrage, exercised in secret, shall not be denied, impeded or otherwise abridged. [69]

7.2 A citizen shall be allowed to vote only in the state where he/she officially resides.

Article 8 Marriage, Divorce, Separation, Annulment, and Adoption.

a. Marriage.

8.1 A marriage shall be a voluntary legal union between two persons no less than eighteen years of age each.

8.2 No one shall be married to more than one person at a time.

8.3 A dowry in any form shall be illegal.

8.4 The right to privacy in a marital relationship shall not be abridged.

8.5 Each marriage shall be formalized in the state district court where the couple gets married.

b. Divorce, Separation, and Annulment.

8.6 Divorce, separation, and annulment shall be governed by the laws of the state where the couple lives, and shall be formalized in the state district court.

8.7 In case of a divorce, a separation or an annulment, the property acquired during the marriage (except for gifts or inheritances) shall be split on a fifty-fifty basis between the spouses. The property acquired before the marriage shall belong to the spouse who acquired it.[70]

c. Adoption.

8.8 An adoption shall be in the best interest of the child being adopted as determined by the state district court, where the adoptive parents reside.

8.9 Adoptive parents shall be citizens of the republic, shall be no less than thirty years of age each, shall be no more than fifty years of age each, and shall be married to each other for no less than five years.

8.10. The adopted child shall be a minor.

8.11 Neither adoptive parents nor adopted child shall be felons.

8.12 Foreign adoptions shall not be allowed.

8.13 Each adoption shall be formalized in the state district court where the adoptive parents live.

8.14. Adoption proceedings shall be confidential, and adoption records shall be sealed.

Article 9 Abortion.

A woman shall have a right to get an abortion as long as it is not used to select the gender of her child.

Article 10. Miscellaneous Illegal Activities.

10.1 Genital mutilation shall be illegal.

10.2 Driving a vehicle, flying an aircraft, or driving a ship or a boat under the influence of a drug or alcohol shall be illegal.

10.3 Disorderly conduct or lewd behavior in public shall be illegal.

10.4 Theft or destruction of public or some one's private property, shall be illegal.

10.5 Killing a person, except in self-defense, as a capital punishment, or in a war, shall be illegal.

10.6 Torture, physical or mental abuse, and assault shall be illegal.

10.7 Participation in money laundering shall be illegal.

10.8 Counterfeiting of official currency shall be illegal.[71]

10.9 Price gouging shall be illegal. The Senate, by an absolute majority vote, shall enact laws necessary to prevent price gouging.

10.10 Perjury shall be illegal.

10.11 Obstruction of justice shall be illegal.

10.12 Planting, destroying, or tampering with trial evidence or witnesses shall be illegal.

10.13 A confidentiality agreement or a nondisclosure contract to silence a victim shall be illegal.

10.14 Forced arbitration shall be illegal.

10.15 Accepting foreign assistance for an election to a public office shall be illegal.

10.16 The use of government facilities and equipment for private gain shall be illegal.

10.17 Entering the republic without a valid visa or a valid passport of the republic shall be illegal.

10.18 Remaining in the republic after one's visa has expired shall be illegal.

10.19 Inciting an illegal activity shall be illegal.

10.20 Ownership of one human being by another shall be illegal.

10.21 Insider trading shall be illegal.

10.22 Child pornography, child endangerment and child abuse shall be illegal.

10.23 Threatening a public official shall be illegal.

10.24 A public vote by proxy shall be illegal.

10.25 Collusion with a foreign entity by a legal resident to undermine the interests of the republic shall be illegal.

Article 11 Ransom.

No government in the republic shall negotiate or pay ransom for the release of any legal resident held as a hostage.

Article 12 Public Funds.

12.1 Only public funds shall be used to pay for the acquisition, operation and maintenance of public facilities. Federal, state, and city governments shall finance acquisition, operation and maintenance of the Senate, the Congress, and the City Council facilities respectively. Federal and state governments shall finance acquisition, operation and maintenance of the federal and the state courts facilities respectively.

12.2 Public funds shall not be used to pay for the misdeeds and illegal activities of any person or entity.

12.3 Only public funds shall be used to finance the top three political parties, as determined by the total number of elected seats in the federal, state and city legislatures in the latest election. If more than one political party has the same number of elected seats in legislatures, the Speaker of the Senate shall cast the tie breaking votes. In absence of an incumbent Speaker, the Vice-President shall cast the tie breaking votes. The eligible candidates of the top three political parties shall not use private funds to finance their election campaigns for a public office. All left over public funds used to finance an election campaign shall be returned to the applicable treasury.

12.4 The federal government shall pay each party the same amount of campaign funds for each incumbent Senator belonging to the party. This amount shall be determined by an absolute majority vote of the Senate.

12.5 Each state government shall pay each party the same amount of campaign funds for each incumbent Congressperson belonging to the party in the state. These amounts shall be determined by an absolute majority vote of each state Congress.

12.6 Each city government shall pay each party the same amount of campaign funds for each incumbent City Council person belonging to the party in the city. These amounts shall be determined by an absolute majority vote of each City Council.

12.7 The leadership of each of the top three political parties shall determine the public funds to be provided to each eligible party candidate running for an election to a public office.

12.8 Public funds shall not be used to provide a loan or a loan guarantee.

12.9 Public funds shall not be used to finance a charity.

12.10 Public funds shall not be used to finance anything religious.

12.11 Public funds shall not be used to finance an election campaign of an independent candidate or of a political party that is not among the top three.

Article 13 Retirement Age.

13.1 No one past his/her seventieth birthday shall be employed by the government or be allowed to work for the government. This shall include both elected and non-elected employees.

13.2 A career civilian employee of the federal, state or city government shall be eligible for retirement and pension at the age of sixty after thirty years of employment with the respective government.

13.3. The military, the police, the national guard, and the fire department personnel shall be eligible for retirement and pension at the age of fifty after twenty five years of service. The mandatory retirement age for such employees shall be sixty years of age.

Article 14 Immigration.

14.1. Immigration into the republic shall be a privilege, not a right.

14.2 Persons meeting the economic demands of the republic, as determined by the federal government, shall be eligible to immigrate to the republic. The spouse and unmarried minor children of a legal immigrant shall be eligible for immigration.

14.3 If a person who is not a legal resident of the republic marries a legal resident of the republic, he/she may be eligible for an immigrant visa.

14.4 Total number of legal immigrants in each profession to be admitted into the country in a given fiscal year shall be determined by a super majority vote of the Senate, during the first month of each fiscal year.

14.5 A point count method approved by a super majority vote of the Senate shall be used as criteria to determine the qualification of a person to immigrate. As a minimum, these criteria shall include professional education, fluency in English, age, and professional experience. The passing grade shall be seventy percent of the maximum possible.

14.6 Immigration into the republic shall be allowed, only when the population density of the republic is no more than sixty persons per square kilometer in the latest census, and shall stop, when it is more than sixty persons per square kilometer in the latest census.[72]

14.7 Economic refugees and illegal immigrants shall not be allowed into the republic. However, in a given fiscal year, political and religious refugees may be allowed, in numbers approved by a super majority vote of the Senate. The number of refugees allocated to a state shall be inversely proportional to the population of the state.

14.8 A child born to a citizen in any part of the world shall be a citizen of the republic. However, a child born to a legal immigrant outside the republic shall only be a legal immigrant to the republic.

14.9 A child born to a legal immigrant inside the republic shall be a citizen of the republic.

14.10 Only a legal resident shall be allowed to work in the republic. Employing a person who is not a legal resident shall be illegal.

14.11 Chain migration shall not be allowed, except as specified in this constitution.

14.12 Immigration to or citizenship of the republic shall not be for sale.

14.13 Immigration or citizenship by lottery shall not be allowed.

14.14 A convicted felon shall not be allowed to immigrate into the republic.

14.15 A legal immigrant who uses public benefits for more than twenty-five percent of the time in any given time period shall lose his/her immigration status.

Article 15 Balanced Budget.

15.1 Every government in the republic shall balance its budget every fiscal year.

15.2 If a balanced budget for the next fiscal year does not become a law by the midnight of the last day of the current fiscal year, the latest legal balanced budget shall go into effect. In absence of such a balanced budget, the total spending of that government shall be frozen at the current fiscal year level until its budget is balanced.

15.3 Any budget surplus shall be used to pay off the government debt. In absence of such debt, it shall be used to reduce the income tax rate until the budget is balanced.

Article 16 Fiscal Year.

A fiscal year shall end at midnight on the thirtieth day of September, and the next fiscal year shall start at the same time.

Article 17 Firearms.

Purchase, ownership, sale and use of firearms shall be a privilege, not a right.[73]

Article 18 Eligibility for a Public Office.

18.1 Only a citizen born in the republic shall be eligible to run for an election or an appointment to a public office.

18.2 No convicted felon shall be allowed to run for an election or an appointment to a public office.

18.3 An individual elected or appointed to a public office shall be required to pass a background check and disclose his/her finances completely before taking office.

18.4 Active duty service in the military for no less than two years with an honorable discharge shall be a necessary condition to run for an election or an appointment to a public office. This clause shall be effective for the following offices after indicated number of years subsequent to the ratification of this constitution: City Councilpersons, Congresspersons and City Political Appointees – 10 years; District Court Judges, Mayors, Deputy Mayors, and State Political Appointees – 15 years; Senators, Governors, Deputy Governors, and Federal Political Appointees – 20 years; Appeals Court Judges – 25 years; Supreme Court Judges, President, and Vice-President – 35 years.

18.5 A candidate running for a Mayor or a Deputy Mayor shall have no less than five years of experience in a City Council or in the state Congress. This clause shall be effective 10 years after the ratification of this constitution.

18.6 A candidate running for the Senate, a Governor or a Deputy Governor shall have no less than five years of experience as a Mayor, or as a Deputy Mayor or no less than ten years of experience as a City Councilperson or as a Congressperson. This clause shall be effective 15 years after the ratification of this constitution.

18.7 A candidate running for a President or a Vice-President shall have no less than fifteen years of experience as a Governor, as a Deputy Governor, or as a Senator. No less than ten years of this experience shall be as a Senator. This clause shall be effective 20 years after the ratification of this constitution.

18.8 Only a college graduate of an accredited university in the republic shall be eligible to run for an election or an appointment to a public office.

18.9 A person shall have lived in a state for no less than three years in order to run in an election for a public office in or from the state.

18.10 A person elected to a public office may run for another public office if eligible. However, no one shall run for or get paid for more than one public office at the same time.

18.11 Any person elected or appointed to a public office shall meet the eligibility criteria for the office specified in this constitution.

18.12 An appointment of an eligible replacement to occupy a vacant seat shall be for the remainder of the term.

Article 19 Work and Pay.

19.1 Equal work shall merit equal pay.

19.2 Full time employment shall consist of no less than 2080 hours of paid work per year.

19.3 Every full-time employee shall be entitled to no less than 160 hours of paid leave per year.

19.4 There shall be no more than ten paid public holidays per year as determined by a super majority vote of the Senate.

Article 20 Government Employment.

20.1 Only a citizen shall be eligible for employment by the government.

20.2 Government employees shall not be allowed to unionize, bargain collectively, or go on a strike.

20.3 No government employee shall be under the influence of alcohol or drugs while on official duty.

20.4 Government employees shall have no external interests that undermine or interfere with their official duties.

20.5 The salary of every government employee shall be determined by law, and shall be adjusted for inflation every fiscal year. No government employee shall be paid more than ten times the median annual household income as determined by the federal government.

20.6 A government employee shall have no other job or business except as specified in this constitution.

20.7 No one shall draw more than one salary from the government.

20.8 No retired government employee shall be allowed to work for the government within three years of his/her retirement.

20.9 No retired government employee shall be allowed to work for his/her contractors within one year of his/her retirement.

20.10 No government employee shall be allowed to work for or lobby the government within three years of his/her departure from it.

20.11 Nepotism or cronyism in the government shall be illegal.

20.12 Using government employment for private gain by an employee or by his/her acquaintances shall be illegal.

20.13 A convicted felon shall not be allowed to work for the government.

20.14 A government employee convicted of felony shall lose his/her job.

20.15 No government employee shall engage in pernicious political activity.[74]

20.16 No government document shall be upclassified retroactively.

20.17 While anonymous whistle blowing about waste, fraud, abuse, corruption, impropriety, or illegal behavior in the government may be allowed, it shall be based on direct, first hand evidence, not on hearsay or secondhand information. The government targeted by the whistle blower shall protect him/her from retribution by the employer.

Article 21 Secret Ballot.

An election to a public office, a referendum, or an initiative shall be voted on by a secret ballot.

Article 22 Life, Liberty, Property and Inheritance Rights.

22.1 Right to life, liberty and property shall not be abridged without due process of law.[75]

22.2 The government shall protect the right of inheritance.[76]

22.3 The estate of a person who dies testate or with a valid will shall be distributed in accordance with his/her will. The estate of person who dies intestate or without a valid will shall be distributed in accordance with the inheritance laws of the state where the person lived at the time of his/her death.

Article 23 Taxes and Dues.

23.1 Each citizen and business shall pay legally established taxes and fees.[77]

23.2 There shall be no taxation without representation.

23.3 All gross incomes shall be taxed at the same rate at a given level of government. The income tax rates for the Federal Government, each state Government, and each city Government shall be decided by the Senate, each state Congress, and each City Council respectively by an absolute majority vote.

23.4 The federal income tax rate shall be greater than the state income tax rate. The state income tax rate shall be greater than the city income tax rate.

23.5 All gross incomes shall be taxed only where they are earned.

23.6 No tax cut shall create, sustain or increase the budget deficit.

23.7 All commerce shall be subject to the local sales tax where goods and services are bought and paid for.

23.8 After a person's death, his/her estate shall be taxed as income. This tax shall be payable before the distribution of the estate according to the person's will or the inheritance laws of the state, as applicable.

23.9 Food, water, and medications shall not be taxed.

23.10 There shall be no tax on the interstate transfer of goods and services. There shall be no tax on the export of goods and services.[78]

Article 24 Treason, Espionage, Terrorism.

Treason, espionage, or terrorism committed against the republic may be punishable by death. A minor committing these acts shall be tried as an adult.

Article 25 Government Functions.

The government shall have three functions: executive, legislative, and judicial. The executive shall enforce the laws, the legislature shall make the laws, and the judiciary shall interpret the laws. Exercise of these functions shall be in accordance with this constitution.

Article 26 Public Office and Religion.

The religious ministers, the judges, the military, the police, the National Guard, and other law enforcement entities as well as civil servants shall be apolitical, and shall neither participate in a political campaign for a public office nor shall be allowed to run for an election to a public office. Similarly, no one elected or appointed to a public office shall be allowed to become a religious minister.[79]

Article 27 Visitors to the Republic.

27.1 A visitor, who is a convicted felon shall not be allowed to enter the republic.

27.2 All visitors to the republic, shall be required to pay for their own health care and medical expenses.

27.3 Any visitor to the republic, who overstays beyond the expiration date of the visa, shall be expelled from the republic forever.

Article 28 Lobbying the Government.

No legal resident shall lobby a government in the republic on behalf of a foreign entity. A legal immigrant who lobbies a government in the republic on behalf of a foreign entity shall lose his/her immigration visa permanently, and shall be expelled from the republic.

Article 29 Negotiating with a Foreign Entity.

Only a federal government employee authorized by the President may negotiate with a foreign entity on behalf of the federal government. No state or city government shall negotiate with a foreign government. No unauthorized person shall negotiate with a foreign government.[80]

Article 30 Government Contracts.

A government contract, as a rule, shall be firm fixed price, and shall be awarded to the qualified bidder with the lowest cost to the government. Any exception to this shall be approved by the head of the applicable department or agency.

Article 31 Private and Religious Institutions.

Private and religious institutions shall not receive any government funds.

Article 32 Financial Institutions.

32.1 Financial institutions, such as, banks and insurance companies shall be regulated by the federal government.

32.2 The securities and the commodities markets shall be regulated by the federal government.

32.3 The functions, responsibilities and authority of insurance industry, commercial banking, and investment banking shall be unique and separate from one another.

32.4 Every account in a commercial bank shall be insured up to a certain amount by the federal government. This amount shall be determined by an absolute majority vote of the Senate.

Article 33 Legal Residents.

Only a legal resident shall be eligible to receive any government benefits.

Article 34 Ratification of this Constitution.

The ratification of this constitution shall require a simple majority of the popular votes cast in a national election with each voter, no less than eighteen years of age, having one up or down vote. After this ratification, any referendum or initiative used to formulate, modify or repeal a law or a public policy shall require no less than a two third majority of the popular votes cast in order to be valid.

Article 35 Amendment of this Constitution.

35.1 To amend this constitution shall require a super majority vote in the Senate plus a super majority of the states casting a super majority vote in each state Congress. The entire amendment process shall take no more than ten years from the first to the last vote, in order to be valid. Each vote shall be an up or down vote, and once cast shall not be changed or rescinded. This constitution shall not be amended by a referendum or an initiative.

35.2 A ratified amendment to this constitution shall become a part of the constitution.

35.3 A secession or autonomy of any territory of the republic or a division or a deletion of a state shall require an amendment to this constitution.

35.4 An addition of a territory to the republic or an addition of a state shall require an amendment to this constitution.

Article 36 Referendum and Initiative.

A referendum shall be supported by no less than thirty percent vote of the Senate, the state Congress or the City Council before it can go on the nationwide, the statewide, or the citywide ballot respectively, for a popular vote. An initiative shall be supported by valid signatures of no less than ten percent of the eligible voters of the country, the state or the city, before it can go on the respective ballot for a popular vote. The latest federal census shall be used to determine the number of eligible voters.

Article 37 Tie Breaking Vote.

37.1 A tie in any vote in the Senate, a Senate election, a national referendum, or a national initiative, shall be broken by the incumbent Speaker of the Senate. In absence of an incumbent Speaker, the Vice-President may cast the tie breaking vote.

37.2 A tie in any vote in a Congress, a Congressional election, a state referendum, or a state initiative, shall be broken by the incumbent Speaker of the Congress of that state. In absence of an incumbent Speaker, the Deputy Governor of the state may cast the tie breaking vote.

37.3 A tie in any vote in a City Council, a City Council election, a city referendum, or a city initiative, shall be broken by the incumbent Speaker of the council of that city. In absence of an incumbent Speaker, the Deputy Mayor of the city may cast the tie breaking vote.

Article 38 Election to a public Office.

38.1 In an election to a public office, the winner(s) shall get a simple majority of the votes cast. If no (pair of) candidate(s) gets a simple majority of the votes cast, the winner(s) shall be decided in a run-off election between the top two (pairs of) candidates. The run-off election shall be held on a weekend two weeks after the results of the first round are final.

38.2 Every election for a public office shall be held at the same time every five years on the first weekend of November.

38.3 Early voting and absentee voting shall be allowed starting four weeks before the election date.

38.4 There shall be no snap elections between scheduled elections.

Article 39 Crime.

A legal resident, who commits a crime in the republic, shall be tried in accordance with the laws of the republic. A legal immigrant, if convicted of a felony in the republic, shall lose his/her immigration status. If a foreigner without a diplomatic immunity commits a crime in the republic, he/she shall be tried in accordance with the laws of the republic, and if convicted, his/her visa shall be revoked. If a foreigner with a diplomatic immunity commits a crime in the republic, his/her diplomatic visa shall be revoked.

Article 40. Public and Private Interests.

In any conflict between public and private interests, the former shall prevail.

Article 41 Sale.

An election or an appointment to a public office shall not be for sale.

Article 42 Citizen.

42.1 Every citizen shall be represented by an elected representative at the federal, state and local levels of government.

42.2 Every citizen shall have the rights and responsibilities of citizenship. No citizen shall be expelled from the republic or shall lose his/her citizenship unwillingly. However, a citizen, who gives up his/her citizenship willingly, shall not get it back. Similarly, an immigrant, who gives up his/her immigrant status willingly, shall not get it back.[81]

42.3 No adult citizen of the republic shall be a citizen of any other country.

Article 43 Population Control.

When the population density of the republic exceeds sixty persons per square kilometer in the latest census, only one child per legal resident couple shall be allowed.

Article 44 Assassination.

An assassination of a law enforcement officer, an active duty military, a National Guard employee, a judge, an elected or an appointed public official shall be punishable by death.

Article 45 Ambassadors.

All ambassadors to foreign countries shall be appointed by the President, and approved by a simple majority vote of the Senate.[82]

Article 46 Census.

The federal government shall conduct a census of citizens every ten years. The number of Senators allocated to a state, the size and shape of Senate districts, Congressional districts, and council districts shall be determined by the results of the census.[83]

Article 47 States.

47.1 The country shall be divided into states of roughly equal sizes of no more than 200,000 square kilometers each.

47.2 Subsequent to addition or deletion of a territory, the resultant territory shall be divided into states of roughly equal sizes.

47.3 The writers of this constitution shall draw the state boundaries with no more than two horizontal and two vertical lines, and no less than one horizontal or one vertical line, in addition to the natural geographical boundaries of the country.

Article 48 Senate Districts.

48.1 The writers of this constitution shall draw the Senate district boundaries with no more than two horizontal and two vertical lines, and no less than one horizontal or one vertical line, in addition to the natural geographical boundaries of the state. After each census, these boundaries shall be redrawn by the Governor of the state in accordance with this rule, and shall be approved by an absolute majority vote of the state Congress.

48.2 Each Senate district in a state shall have roughly the same number of citizens, and shall be represented by a Senator.

Article 49 Congressional Districts.

49.1 The writers of this constitution shall draw the Congressional district boundaries with no more than two horizontal and two vertical lines, and no less than one horizontal or one vertical line, in addition to the natural geographical boundaries of the state. After each census, these boundaries shall be redrawn by the Governor of the state in accordance with this rule, and shall be approved by an absolute majority vote of the state Congress.

49.2 Each Congressional district in a state shall have roughly the same number of citizens, and shall be represented by a Congressperson.

Article 50 City.

The area of a city shall be no less than 100 square kilometers and no more than 1600 square kilometers with a population density of no less than 1500 persons per square kilometer. The writers of this constitution shall draw the city boundaries with no more than two horizontal and two vertical lines, and no less than one horizontal or one vertical line, in addition to the natural geographical boundaries of the state. After each census, these boundaries shall be redrawn by the Governor of the state in accordance with this rule, and shall be approved by an absolute majority vote of the state Congress.

Article 51 City Council Districts.

51.1 The writers of this constitution shall draw the city council district boundaries with no more than two horizontal and two vertical lines, and no less than one horizontal or one vertical line, in addition to the natural geographical boundaries of the city. After each census, these boundaries shall be redrawn by the Mayor of the city, and shall be approved by an absolute majority vote of the City Council.

51.2 Each council district in a city shall have roughly the same number of citizens, and shall be represented by a Councilperson.

Article 52 Slavery and Serfdom.

Slavery and serfdom shall be illegal in the republic.

Article 53 Involuntary Servitude and Indentured Labor.

53.1 Involuntary servitude shall be illegal in the republic except as a result of the due legal process.[84]

53.2 Indentured labor shall be illegal.

Article 54 Usury.

Usury shall be illegal in the republic. The usurious interest rate for a fiscal year shall be determined by an absolute majority vote of the Senate during the first month of each fiscal year.

Article 55 Child labor.

Child labor shall be illegal in the republic. Anyone less than sixteen years of age shall be considered a child.

Article 56 Sex.

56.1 All involuntary sex, including rapes and sexual assault, shall be illegal.

56.2 Sexual harassment, irrespective of the gender and sexual preferences of the parties involved, shall be illegal.

56.3 Any sexual activity with a minor shall be illegal.

Article 57 Minor.

A minor indicted for committing a murder shall be tried as an adult.

Article 58 Debt.

58.1 No debt owed to the government shall be forgiven.

58.2 Private losses and debts shall not be paid for by the government.

Article 59 Prostitution.

Prostitution, human trafficking, and child pornography shall be illegal.

Article 60 Statues and Monuments.

60.1 There shall be no public statues or monuments of living persons. No public property shall be named after a living person.

60.2 Constructing a public statue or a monument of a dead person or naming a public property after a dead person shall be approved by a super majority vote of the Senate.

60.3 Removing a public statue or a monument or the name of a dead person from a public property shall be approved by a super majority vote of the Senate.

Article 61 Bribe.

61.1 Bribing a foreigner in cash or in kind by a legal resident of the republic shall be illegal.

61.2 Bribing a government employee in cash or in kind shall be as illegal as acceptance of that bribe by a government employee.

Article 62 Lean and Six Sigma.

62.1 The efficiency of the government processes shall be improved by reducing waste through the use of lean methodology.

62.2 Each government department and agency shall return a percentage of its operating budget as determined by an absolute majority vote of the corresponding legislature each fiscal year to the corresponding treasury by reducing waste through lean.

62.3 The variation in the products and services offered by the government shall be reduced by using the six-sigma methodology.

62.4 The Vice-President at the federal level, the Deputy Governor at the state level, and the Deputy Mayor at the city level shall be responsible for the implementation of lean and six-sigma.

Article 63 Poverty.

The official poverty level shall be defined as half of the median annual household income.

Article 64 Annual Compensation.

The total annual compensation of a private sector employee shall not exceed one hundred times the median annual household income as determined by the federal government. This limit shall not apply to self-employed people.

Article 65 Seat of the Government.

65.1 The capital of the republic shall be the seat of the federal government.

65.2 The capital of each state shall be the seat of the state government.

Article 66 Visa.

66.1 The federal government shall be responsible for issuing all visas.

66.2 A student visa shall be issued for a period of one year to each foreign student admitted to study in an accredited university in the republic. It shall be renewable every year until the student graduates from the university.

66.3 A visitor visa or a business visa shall last for three months. The business visa may be renewed for a period of three months from the person's point of origin. The visitor visa may be renewed once a year for a period of three months from the person's point of origin.

66.4 A diplomatic visa shall be issued to a foreign diplomat for a period of one year. It shall be renewable yearly until the official departure of the diplomat.

66.5 An immigration visa shall be issued to qualified candidates, who shall report their official residence to the federal government every year.

Article 67 Accounting system.

Every government organization, agency and department shall have an accounting system that can be audited independently every fiscal year. An independent audit of every government organization, agency, and department shall be conducted every fiscal year with the results made publicly available.

Article 68 Habeas Corpus.

The suspension of Habeas Corpus in cases of rebellion or invasion that threaten the public safety shall require a super majority vote in the Senate, and shall not exceed 52 weeks.[85]

Article 69 Campaign Contributions.

69.1 All campaign contributions shall be publicly reported, and shall be subject to an independent audit by the applicable government.

69.2 Only citizens of the republic shall be allowed to contribute their resources to a political party or to a candidate running for a public office in an election campaign.

Article 70 Appropriations Law.

The only authority for withdrawing money from the treasury shall be the appropriations law. The records of revenues and expenditures shall be public.[86]

Article 71 Metric system.

71.1 The republic shall use the international metric system for measurements.

71.2 The republic shall use a twenty-four-hour clock for measuring time.

Article 72 Election Campaign.

Neither an election campaign for a political office nor the public financing for it shall start more than ninety days before the official election date.

Article 73 Legislative Inquiry.

73.1 No legislative inquiry or investigation shall be open ended in terms of the resources required. Every inquiry shall have a charter, a schedule and a budget approved by an absolute majority vote of the investigating legislature. Any modification to this charter, schedule or budget shall be approved by a super majority vote of the investigating legislature. The inquiry shall be conducted for no more than eight hours per day, forty hours per week, allowing one hour for lunch every day. No inquiry shall be conducted on Saturday or Sunday. Unless prohibited by a super majority vote of the legislature, a legislative inquiry or investigation shall be open to the public. The investigating legislature shall pay the relevant expenses of people required to testify in an inquiry.

73.2 The scope of legislative oversight of the executive shall be specified in a law passed by a supermajority vote of that legislature.

73.3 The federal government shall create and save verbatim records of the Presidential meetings and communications with foreign leaders. A supermajority vote of the senate shall be required for it to access any of these records.

73.4 Each political party in a legislature shall be represented proportionately in every legislative committee in that legislature. The chairperson of the committee shall be elected by a simple majority vote of the committee.

73.5 Impeachable offences shall be specified in a law passed by a super majority vote of the Senate.

Article 74 Public Office Candidate.

The leadership of a political party shall choose the candidate who will run for a given public office on the party ticket. It shall also have the authority to prevent a person from running on the party ticket or to discipline a person including expelling him/her from the party.

Article 75 Treaty.

75.1 The federal government shall have the sole authority to enter into a treaty, an agreement, a contract or an alliance with a foreign government, to coin money, to impose duty or excise tax on imported goods, and to engage in a war.[87]

75.2 The republic shall not enter into or exit from a treaty, an agreement, a contract or an alliance with a foreign government without approval by a super majority vote of the Senate.

75.3 Any treaty or contract between states shall be approved by an absolute majority vote of each Congress of the involved states, and shall be signed by the Governors of these states. Additionally, it shall be approved by an absolute majority vote of the Senate and signed by the President. The same procedure shall apply to changing/repealing a treaty or a contract between the states. [88]

75.4 Any treaty or contract between the federal government and states shall be approved by an absolute majority vote of the Senate and the Congress of each of these states, and shall be signed by the President and the Governors of these states. The same procedure shall apply to changing/repealing a treaty or a contract between the federal government and states.

Article 76 Extradition.

76.1 A citizen of the republic shall not be expelled from the republic, but may be extradited subject to the conditions specified in this constitution.

76.2 A citizen of the republic, who has committed a crime in a foreign country, and whose extradition is requested by that country, may be extradited to that country, if the republic has signed a reciprocal extradition treaty with that country covering this kind of extradition, and if the extradition is unanimously approved by the federal Supreme Court. An immigrant in this situation shall be returned to his/her country of origin, and if convicted of felony, shall lose his/her immigration status permanently.

76.3 A legal resident of the republic, who has violated the law of the republic, and has sought refuge in a foreign country, shall be extradited from that country, if the republic has an extradition treaty with that country. An immigrant in this situation, if convicted of a crime shall lose his/her immigration status permanently

76.4 If a foreign visitor has violated the laws of a country that seeks his/her extradition, he/she shall be returned to his/her country of origin.

Article 77 Liability for Official Acts.

The executive, the legislative, and the judiciary members shall not be held liable for acts performed in the exercise of their official duties.[89] However, they may be sued for actions unrelated to their official duties.

Article 78 Currency.

The republic shall have a convertible currency pegged to a precious metal, such as gold or silver.

Article 79 Personnel Cost.

79.1 All the government personnel cost, including the salaries, the health care, and the retirement pension shall be part of the department or agency budget for which these personnel work.

79.2 No public retirement pension system or social security funds in the republic shall have an unfunded liability.

79.3 The public retirement pension funds, the social security funds, and the government budget shall be kept separate from one another.

Article 80 Intellectual Property.

All intellectual property shall be protected in accordance with the international agreement on Trade Related Aspects of Intellectual Property Rights (TRIPS) administered by the World Trade Organization (WTO).[90]

Article 81 Eminent Domain.

The Government shall have a right to seize private property solely for public use, if it pays fair market value to the owner of the property.[91]

Article 82 Nuclear Energy.

The Federal Government shall establish standards for and regulate the production and utilization of nuclear energy.[92]

Article 83 Transportation.

The Federal Government shall establish standards for transportation via air, land, water, and space. The regulation of inter-state, intra-state, and intra-city transportation in accordance with these standards shall be the responsibility of the Federal, the applicable State, and the applicable City Governments respectively.[93]

Article 84 Privacy, Cybersecurity, E-commerce, Mail and Telecommunications.

The Federal Government shall establish standards and regulations regarding privacy, cybersecurity, e-commerce, mail, and telecommunications services.[94]

Article 85 Waterways and Water Reservoirs.

The Federal Government shall establish standards for waterways and water reservoirs. The regulation of inter-state, intra-state, and intra-city waterways and water reservoirs in accordance with these standards shall be the responsibility of the Federal, the applicable state, and the applicable city Governments respectively.[95]

Article 86 Roads and Highways.

The Federal Government shall establish standards for roads and highways. The regulation of inter-state, intra-state, and intra-city roads and highways in accordance with these standards shall be the responsibility of the Federal, the applicable State, and the applicable City Governments respectively.[96]

Article 87 Information Technology.

The Federal Government shall establish standards for and regulate the Information Technology devices, networks, security and communications in accordance with these standards.[97]

Article 88 Hazardous Materials (HAZMAT).

The Federal Government shall establish standards for and regulate the safe storage and transfer of Hazardous Materials (HAZMAT) in accordance with these standards.

Article 89 Environment.

The Federal Government shall establish standards for and regulate the protection of environment in accordance with these standards.

Article 90. Food Safety.

The federal Government shall establish standards for and regulate the safety of food, pharmaceutical drugs, and cosmetics in accordance with these standards.

Article 91 Consumer Safety.

The Federal Government shall establish standards for and regulate consumer product safety in accordance with these standards.

Article 92 Health Care.

92.1 Every legal resident shall have an option to buy the health insurance provided by the federal government at the annual premium per household of no more than five percent of the median annual household income.

92.2 The Federal Government shall provide recommendations and establish guidelines and requirements for administering the prevention of diseases and impairments, and promotion of health and well-being.

Chapter II: The Executive Function

A. General.

Article 93 The Executive Term.

93.1 The executive term shall start at noon on the twentieth day of January immediately following the election of legislatures. Each legislature shall elect the corresponding executive on or before noon on that day.

93.2 No person shall be elected as a President, a Vice-President, a Governor, a Deputy Governor, a Mayor or a Deputy Mayor for more than two five-year terms before the mandatory retirement age of seventy for government employees.

93.3 A person who has served as a President for two elected five-year terms shall not be allowed to become a President. A person who has served as a Governor for two elected five-year terms shall not be allowed to become a Governor. A person who has served as a Mayor for two elected five-year terms shall not be allowed to become a Mayor.

Article 94 The Executive Address.

On the first Tuesday of February every year, the President shall give a state of the republic address to the Senate.[98] On the second Tuesday of February every year, each Governor shall give a state of the state address to the state Congress. On the third Tuesday of February every year, each Mayor shall give a state of the city address to the City Council. None of these addresses shall last for more than an hour, and shall focus on goals and priorities of the administration for the coming calendar year along with the accomplishments of the last calendar year in relation to the goals set.

Article 95 The Executive Age.

At the time of being sworn into the office, a Mayor and a Deputy Mayor shall be no less than thirty years of age each; a Governor and a Deputy Governor shall be no less than thirty-five years of age each; a President and a Vice-President shall be no less than fifty years of age each.

Article 96 The Executive Cabinet.

96.1 The President, the Governor, and the Mayor shall form their cabinets from the elected incumbents in the respective legislatures. The appointed cabinet members shall also continue to perform their legislative duties as representatives of their constituents in addition to managing the assigned departments. They shall be appointed by the executive and shall be confirmed by a simple majority vote of the corresponding legislature. Every appointee shall be judged on the basis of his/her competence for the job and character. The confirmation process shall take no more than thirty business days. If the appointee is neither confirmed nor rejected during this time period, he/she shall be considered confirmed by default. If he/she is rejected, the entire process shall be repeated with a different appointee.

96.2 A super majority vote of a legislature shall be required to remove a corresponding cabinet member in an up or down vote.

Article 97 Law Enforcement.

97.1 Only a public official legally authorized and paid to enforce the law shall enforce the law. Vigilantism, posse comitatus, or civilians taking law in their hands shall be illegal.

97.2 Law enforcement including the prison system shall not be privatized.

97.3 Law enforcement officials in a given Senate, Congress or City Council district shall reflect the local demographics based on the latest census.

Article 98 Executive Limit.

98.1 No executive shall perform a judicial function.

98.2 No executive shall suspend, dismiss or break up a legislature or a judiciary.

A. Federal.

Article 99 The President and the Vice-President.

99.1 The chief executive of the federal government shall be the President,[99] who shall also be the commander in chief of the armed forces[100], responsible for the defense of this constitution, maintenance of law and order within the country, and the sovereignty and the territorial integrity of the republic from external and internal threats.[101]

99.2 The President and the Vice-President of the republic shall be elected as a pair by the Senate for a period of five years with a simple majority vote. They shall be incumbent Senators from the same political party, and shall continue to perform their duties as Senators.

99.3 Before entering the office of the Presidency, the President shall take the following oath: "I do solemnly swear that I will faithfully execute the Office of the President of the Republic, and will to the best of my ability, preserve, protect, and defend the Constitution of the Republic."[102] The Chief Justice of the Republic shall administer this oath.

Article 100 Replacing the President and the Vice-President.

100.1 In case of unwillingness or inability of the President to serve as the President, or if the President is removed from the office by a supermajority vote of the Senate, or if the President retires, the Vice-President shall become the new President.[103] The new Vice-President, belonging to the same political party, shall be elected from the Senate by a simple majority vote of the Senate.

100.2 In case of unwillingness or inability of the Vice-President to serve as the Vice-President, or if the Vice-President is removed from the office by a supermajority vote of the Senate, or if the Vice-President retires, the new Vice-President, belonging to the same political party, shall be elected from the Senate by a simple majority vote of the Senate.

100.3 In case of unwillingness or inability of the President and the Vice-President to serve as the President and the Vice-President, or if they are removed from their offices by a supermajority vote of the Senate, or if they retire, the new President and the new Vice-President, belonging to the same political party, shall be elected from the Senate by a simple majority vote of the Senate.

Article 101 A Vote of No Confidence in the Senate.

No more than one vote of no confidence shall be allowed at any level of government in a period of five years.

A vote of no confidence in the federal government shall require a super majority vote in the Senate. Once the Senate passes the vote of no confidence, the President, the Vice-President, and all the Cabinet Secretaries shall resign their positions in the government. They shall retain their jobs as Senators. A new President and a new Vice-President from the same political party shall be elected as a pair by a simple majority vote of the Senate. Any Senator eligible to become a President or a Vice-President shall be allowed to run for these offices. If no pair gets a simple majority vote in the Senate, there shall be a run-off election between the top two pairs. The pair that gets the simple majority vote in the Senate, shall become the new President and the new Vice-President. The new President shall select the new Cabinet Secretaries, who, once confirmed by a simple majority vote of the Senate, shall form the new government.

Article 102 Martial law.

In case of national emergency, a martial law may be declared by the President, for no more than ninety days, subject to an approval by a super majority vote of the Senate. The martial law shall specify the authority and the responsibilities of the President during the martial law.

Article 103 Executive Order.

103.1 Only a President shall have an authority to issue an executive order.

103.2 No President shall issue more than three executive orders per fiscal year.

103.3 No executive order issued by the President shall last for more than thirty days.

103.4 No part of an executive order shall be reissued, except as a legislative statute.

103.5 No part of an executive order shall duplicate, amend, repeal, supersede, or contradict any part of this constitution or any existing federal statute.

Article 104 Undesirable Alien.

The President may deport any non-citizen as an undesirable alien, if there is a probable cause for his/her deportation.

Article 105 Foreign and Domestic Policy.

The President, as the head of the republic, shall be responsible for the foreign as well as the domestic policy of the republic.[104]

Article 106 Federal Election Commission.

Ninety days before each official election date, the President shall appoint an independent Federal Election Commission that will be responsible for ensuring a fair and a free election. This commission shall be dismantled once the election results are final.

B. State.

Article 107 The Governor and the Deputy Governor.

107.1 The chief executive of a state shall be the Governor, who shall be responsible for the maintenance of law and order within his/her state with the help of the state police and the National Guard under his/her command.

107.2 A super majority vote of the state congress shall be required for the Governor to deploy the National Guard.

107.3 The Governor and the Deputy Governor of a state shall be elected as a pair by the Congress of the state for a period of five years with a simple majority vote. They shall be incumbent Congresspersons from the same political party, and shall continue to perform their duties as Congresspersons.

Article 108 Replacing the Governor and the Deputy Governor.

108.1 In case of unwillingness or inability of the Governor to serve as the Governor, or if the Governor is removed from the office by a supermajority vote of the Congress, or if the Governor retires, the Deputy Governor shall become the new Governor. A new Deputy Governor, belonging to the same political party, shall be elected from the Congress by a simple majority vote of the Congress.

108.2 In case of unwillingness or inability of the Deputy Governor to serve as the Deputy Governor, or if a Deputy Governor is removed from the office by a supermajority vote of the Congress, or if a Deputy Governor retires, a new Deputy Governor, belonging to the same political party, shall be elected from the Congress by a simple majority vote of the Congress.

108.3 In case of unwillingness or inability of the Governor and the Deputy Governor to serve as the Governor and the Deputy Governor, or if they are removed from their offices by a supermajority vote of the Congress, or if they retire, a new Governor and a new Deputy Governor, belonging to the same political party, shall be elected from the Congress by a simple majority vote of the Congress.

Article 109 A Vote of No Confidence in a State Congress.

A vote of no confidence in the state government shall require a super majority vote in the Congress of that state. Once the Congress passes the vote of no confidence, the Governor, the Deputy Governor, and all the Cabinet Secretaries shall resign their positions in the government. They shall retain their jobs as Congresspersons. A new Governor and a new Deputy Governor from the same political party shall be elected as a pair by a simple majority vote of the Congress. Any Congressperson eligible to become a Governor or a Deputy Governor shall be allowed to run for these offices. If no pair gets a simple majority vote in the Congress, there shall be a run-off election between the top two pairs. The pair that gets the simple majority vote in the Congress, shall become the new Governor and the new Deputy Governor. The new Governor shall select the new Cabinet Secretaries, who, once confirmed by a simple majority vote of the Congress, shall form the new government.

C. City.

Article 110. The Mayor and the Deputy Mayor.

110.1 The chief executive of a city shall be a Mayor, who shall be responsible for the maintenance of law and order within his/her city with the help of the city police under his/her command.

110.2 The Mayor and the Deputy Mayor of a city shall be elected as a pair by the City Council for a period of five years with a simple majority vote. They shall be incumbent City Councilpersons from the same political party, and shall continue to perform their duties as City Councilpersons.

Article 111 Replacing the Mayor and the Deputy Mayor.

111.1 In case of unwillingness or inability of the Mayor to serve as the Mayor, or if the Mayor is removed from the office by a supermajority vote of the City Council, or if the Mayor retires, the Deputy Mayor shall become the new Mayor. A new Deputy Mayor, belonging to the same political party, shall be elected from the City Council by a simple majority vote of the City Council.

111.2 In case of unwillingness or inability of the Deputy Mayor to serve as the Deputy Mayor, or if the Deputy Mayor is removed from the office by a supermajority vote of the City Council, or if the Deputy Mayor retires, a new Deputy Mayor, belonging to the same political party, shall be elected from the council by a simple majority vote of the City Council.

111.3 In case of unwillingness or inability of the Mayor and the Deputy Mayor to serve as the Mayor and the Deputy Mayor, or if they are removed from their offices by a supermajority vote of the City Council, or if they retire, a new Mayor and a new Deputy Mayor, belonging to the same political party, shall be elected from the City Council by a simple majority vote of the City Council.

Article 112 A Vote of No Confidence in a City Council.

A vote of no confidence in the city government shall require a super majority vote in the City Council of that city. Once the City Council passes the vote of no confidence, the Mayor, the Deputy Mayor, and all the Cabinet Secretaries shall resign their positions in the government. They shall retain their jobs as City Councilpersons. A new Mayor and a new Deputy Mayor from the same political party shall be elected as a pair by a simple majority vote of the City Council. Any City Councilperson eligible to become a Mayor or a Deputy Mayor shall be allowed to run for these offices. If no pair gets a simple majority vote in the City Council, there shall be a run-off election between the top two pairs. The pair that gets the simple majority vote in the City Council, shall become the new Mayor and the new Deputy Mayor. The new Mayor shall select the new Cabinet Secretaries, who, once confirmed by a simple majority vote of the City Council, shall form the new government

Chapter III: The Legislative Function.

A. General.

Article 113 Senate, Congress, and City Council.

113.1 The federal legislature shall be called the Senate, the state legislature shall be called a Congress, and the city legislature shall be called a City Council.

113.2 Each Senator, Congressperson and City Councilperson shall have one vote in the respective legislative chamber.

113.3 Each legislature shall adjourn for recess during the month of August.

Article 114 Compensation and Pay Raises.

114.1 No government employee shall be paid more than a Senator.

114.2 A Senator shall be paid more than a Congressperson. A Congressperson shall be paid more than a City Councilperson.

114.3 Every legislator in the same legislature shall have the same salary.

114.4 A super majority vote of a legislature shall be required to pass a proposed legislative pay raise.

114.5 A proposed legislative pay raise shall not be effective until after the next election.[105]

Article 115 Laws or Statutes.

115.1 Senate, Congress and City Council shall pass statutes covering matters within their respective jurisdictions. Rules and regulations issued by each government shall be derived from the statutes passed by the corresponding legislature.[106] Each rule and regulation shall specify the statute it is based on, and shall be subject to an annual independent audit to verify that each rule and regulation is based on a statute.

115.2 Statutes shall be concise, clear, consistent, easy to understand, and detailed enough to cover all eventualities. They shall be continually updated and codified. Difficult terms shall be explained in a glossary.

115.3 Each law shall address a specific issue, and shall stand on its own merit. Unrelated issues shall not be combined in a single piece of legislation.

115.4 A money (i.e., a taxing or a spending) bill shall not be combined with a non-money bill.[107]

115.5 No law shall be enacted to last for more than fifty years. The sunset date for each law shall be specified in the law.

115.6 No law enacted by a legislature shall duplicate or contradict any other law enacted by the same legislature.

115.7 Laws shall be enacted and implemented with a view to establish and maintain a just, a fair, and an equitable society.

115.8 No law shall be enacted or implemented retroactively.[108]

115.9 No legislature in the republic shall pass a law violating, contradicting or undermining any part of this constitution.

115.10 Each legislature shall provide the resources necessary to implement the laws it enacts in order to ensure that no unfunded mandate is passed on to any part of the government as a result of the law.

115.11 A super majority vote of a legislature shall be required to enact a victimless crime law.

115.12 The Senate shall enact laws to prevent business monopolies, to promote competition, and to discourage quotas.[109]

115.13 The Senate shall enact laws to regulate interstate commerce and commerce with foreign countries.[110]

115.14 The Senate, by an absolute majority vote, shall determine as to (a) which illegal activities are civil offenses, and which ones are criminal offenses, and (b) which criminal offenses are misdemeanors, and which ones are felonies.

115.15 The Senate shall pass a law identifying situations that require a written contract in order to be legally enforceable.

115.16 The Senate shall pass a body of laws covering all the commercial issues, such as sales and warranties.

Article 116 Minimum Wages, Unemployment Benefits, Government Pensions, and Social Security.

Applicable legislatures, by an absolute majority vote, shall establish minimum wages, unemployment benefits, government pensions, and social security benefits for legal residents who are no less than sixty five years of age or are disabled or are minor orphans or are widows or widowers with dependent children.[111] These amounts shall be adjusted for inflation in the first month of every fiscal year, and shall be enough to live on.

Article 117 The legislative Term.

117.1 The legislative term shall start at noon on the twentieth day of January immediately following the legislative elections.

117.2 A Senator shall be elected for five years by the eligible voters of a Senate district. A Congressperson shall be elected for five years by the eligible voters of a Congressional district. A City Councilperson shall be elected for five years by the eligible voters of a City Council district.

Article 118 Legislative Age limits.

A City Councilperson and a Congressperson shall be no less than twenty-five years of age each, and a Senator shall be no less than thirty-five years of age.

Article 119 Speaker.

119.1 Each legislature shall elect a Speaker for the legislative term by a simple majority vote. A tie vote in electing a Speaker shall be broken by the vote of the preceding Speaker in the corresponding legislature. The Speaker shall plan, schedule, regulate, and preside over the reading and debating of each bill. He/she shall rule on points of order and the conduct of members. The Speaker shall not participate in debates, shall always act politically impartial, and shall vote in order to break a tie in addition to casting a vote as a legislator.[112]

119.2 The speaker of each legislature shall be responsible for timely public disclosure of misdeeds and illegal activities of its members. The chief executive of each legislature shall be responsible for timely disclosure of misdeeds and illegal activities of its speaker.

Article 120 Submitting a Bill to the Speaker.

For a bill to be formally submitted by a legislator to the Speaker, it shall have a sponsor and no less than two cosponsors from the same legislature as the Speaker and the legislator.

Article 121 Gerrymandering.

Gerrymandering, defined as the practice of redrawing electoral districts to gain an electoral advantage for a political party, shall be illegal.

Article 122 Voting in Person.

Every vote cast in a legislature by a legislator shall be cast in person, in order to be valid.[113]

Article 123 Legislative Sessions.

123.1 All legislative sessions shall be public, and shall be officially documented and published verbatim as a matter of public record, unless they are classified for national security reasons.[114]

123.2 A super majority of a legislature shall be in attendance in the legislative chamber in order for legislators to conduct official business.[115]

Article 124 Rules.

124.1 No rule made by a legislature for its internal functioning shall violate the majority rule of a democracy.[116]

124.2 No rule shall undermine the legislative process.

Article 125 Revenues, Expenditures, Taxes, and Budgets.

The Senate shall be responsible for the revenues, expenditures, creating official currency, taxes, duties, tariffs, excise, borrowing, paying the debt, providing for the defense, and the budget of the republic. The Congress shall be responsible for the revenues, expenditures, taxes, borrowing, paying the debt, and the budget of the state, and the City Council shall be responsible for the revenues, expenditures, taxes, borrowing, paying the debt, and the budget of the city.[117]

Article 126 Subpoena.

An absolute majority vote of District Court judges shall be required in order for them to issue a subpoena.

Article 127 Legislative Limit.

127.1 No legislator shall perform a judicial function except as specified in this constitution.

127.2 No legislature shall pass a law punishing a legal resident without a trial.[118]

Article 128 A Bill becoming a Law.

A bill passed by an absolute majority vote of a legislature shall be sent to the corresponding executive for signature. The executive shall either sign the bill as presented, to make it a law or veto the bill, partially or completely, with specific objections, in no more than ten business days from the day of receipt from the legislature. If the bill is neither signed nor vetoed in ten business days, it shall become the law. If the bill is vetoed, it shall go back to the legislature. The legislature shall have no more than ten business days from the day of receipt from the executive either to override the veto by a super majority vote or to accept the veto, and send the resultant bill back to the executive for signature. The executive shall have no more than ten business days from the day of receipt from the legislature to sign the resultant bill. Whether the executive signs the bill or not, it shall become the law after ten business days. A super majority vote of a legislature on a bill shall be immune from the executive veto.[119]

Article 129 A Whip.

Each political party in a legislature shall elect a Whip to exercise the party discipline.

Article 130. Reading of a Bill.

Each bill shall be read aloud three times in the legislature before it can be voted on. The first reading shall be purely formal with no debates. The second reading shall involve debates on the principles of the bill. The bill shall then go to the appropriate committee for clause by clause examination and markup. The markup shall then go to the legislature for the third reading and debates. The bill shall be completely read aloud in the legislature. The amended or final bill shall then be voted on by the legislature.[120]

Article 131 Removal and Replacement of a Legislator.

131.1 A super majority vote of a legislature shall be required to remove a legislator from the same legislature.[121]

131.2 If a legislator is unable or unwilling to serve in the legislature, or if a legislator is removed by a supermajority vote of the legislature, or if a legislator retires, the Speaker of that legislature shall find an eligible replacement from the same political party, and the same legislative district as the incumbent legislator. If the incumbent legislator is an independent, i.e., not affiliated with a political party, the replacement shall belong to the same political party as the corresponding executive.

Article 132 Removal and Replacement of a Speaker.

132.1 A super majority vote of a legislature shall be required to remove a Speaker from the same legislature

132.2 If a Speaker is unable or unwilling to serve as a Speaker, or if a Speaker is removed by a supermajority vote of the legislature, or if a Speaker retires, the corresponding legislature shall elect a new Speaker, belonging to the same political party, by a simple majority vote. If the incumbent Speaker is an independent, i.e., not affiliated with a political party, the Speaker replacement shall belong to the same political party as the corresponding executive.

Article 133 The Government Shutdown.

If the government employees do not get paid as a result of the government shutdown caused by the legislature, neither shall the legislature get paid, as long as the shutdown lasts.

B. Federal.

Article 134 Number of Senators per State.

The number of Senators allocated to a state shall be directly proportional to the number of citizens in the state as determined by the latest census. The average number of Senators per state shall be ten. However, no state shall have less than one Senator. Initially, the writers of this constitution, and then, the Vice-President shall determine the number of Senators in each state in accordance with this rule.

Article 135 Declaring or ending a War.

135.1 Only the Senate shall have the power to declare a war against a foreign country. A war resolution, to be made public, shall specify as to why it is in the interest of the republic to fight the war.[122] The republic shall not fight an undeclared war under any pretext.

135.2 To declare or end a war against a foreign country, or to approve a treaty or an agreement with a foreign country shall require a super majority vote of the Senate in an up or down vote, with no amendments, in no more than four weeks after the Presidential request to the Senate.[123]

Article 136 Federal Reserve Bank.

The Senate shall be responsible for establishing an independent Federal Reserve Bank headed by a chairperson. The chairperson shall be appointed by the President for a period of ten years with the consent of a simple majority vote of the Senate. A super majority vote of the Senate shall be required to remove the chairperson. The Federal Reserve Bank shall determine the monetary policy, and the money supply, in order to influence interest rates and ensure non-inflationary growth of the economy.

Article 137 Replacement of the Entire Senate.

If the entire Senate is killed or incapacitated at a given time, the Governor of each state shall replace each Senator from his/her state with an eligible candidate from the same Senate district and of the same political party as the incumbent for the remainder of the term. The new Senate shall then elect the new President, the Vice-President and the Speaker of the Senate for the remainder of the term.

C. State.

Article 138 Number of Congresspersons.

The number of Congresspersons in a state shall be directly proportional to the number of citizens in the state as determined by the latest census. The least populated state shall have twenty-five, and the most populated state shall have one hundred Congresspersons. Initially, the writers of this constitution, and then, the Deputy Governor of the state shall determine the number of Congresspersons in the state in accordance with this rule.

Article 139 Replacement of the Entire State Congress.

If the entire Congress of a state is killed or incapacitated at a given time, the President shall replace each Congressperson with an eligible candidate from the same Congressional district and of the same political party as the incumbent for the remainder of the term. The new Congress shall then elect the new Governor, the Deputy Governor, and the Speaker of the Congress for the remainder of the term.

D. City.

Article 140. Number of Councilpersons.

The number of Councilpersons in a city shall be directly proportional to the number of citizens in the city as determined by the latest census. The least populated city shall have twenty-five, and the most populated city shall have fifty Councilpersons. Initially, the writers of this constitution, and then, the Deputy Mayor of the city shall determine the number of Councilpersons in each city in accordance with this rule.

Article 141 Replacement of the Entire Council.

If the entire City Council is killed or incapacitated at a given time, the Governor of the state shall replace each City Councilperson with an eligible candidate from the same City Council district and of the same political party as the incumbent for the remainder of the term. The new

City Council shall then elect the new Mayor, the Deputy Mayor, and the Speaker of the City Council for the remainder of the term.

Chapter IV: The Judicial Function

A. General.

Article 142 Judicial Decisions.

142.1 Except in interpreting this constitution, a judicial decision shall be based primarily on a statute, and secondarily on a legal precedent or a norm or a custom, if no statute is available.

142.2 A statute shall override a legal precedent or a norm or a custom.[124]

142.3 A judicial decision based on a legal precedent or a norm or a custom shall be promptly enacted into a statute by the applicable legislature.

Article 143 Judicial Oversight.

The Federal Appellate Courts shall provide the judicial oversight over the legality and constitutionality of an executive or a legislative action within the republic. The State Appellate Courts shall provide the judicial oversight over the legality and constitutionality of an executive or a legislative action within the state.

Article 144 The Judiciary.

144.1 The judiciary shall be divided into the district court, the appeals court and the Supreme Court in an ascending order of priority at the federal and the state level. Each Court shall have responsibility and authority necessary to discharge the judiciary function within its jurisdiction. For federal courts, this shall extend to all cases involving the laws of the republic, maritime jurisdiction, controversies involving the republic, controversies involving states, between a state and residents of another state or country, or between any part of the republic and a foreign country.[125] For state courts, this shall extend to all cases involving the laws of the state.

144.2 The judges shall be the main investigators. They shall conduct majority of the trial instead of allowing cross-examination between the defense and the prosecution as in the British Common Law. The legal system shall be inquisitorial as in France and Germany rather than adversarial as in the U.S., the U.K., Australia and New Zealand. In District Courts, the judges shall be actively involved in conducting the case by directly questioning the witnesses to establish the facts of the case, and shall apply the provisions of the applicable statutes. During the trial, the parties shall give all their evidence to the judges, who will then call forward and question the witnesses, after which the defense counsel and the prosecutor may question the witnesses. District courts shall decide cases on the basis of the facts and the law.[126]

144.3 The prosecutor shall conduct a pre-trial investigation, shall decide whether to press a charge against the defendant or to drop it, and shall represent the government in a criminal case. He/she shall not withhold exculpatory evidence, and shall make it available to the defense in order to promote justice. If he/she is convinced of the defendant's innocence, he/she shall plead in favor of the defendant.[127]

144.4 The prosecutor shall collect both inculpatory and exculpatory evidence. The defendant shall not have to provide proof of his/her innocence, and shall not be obliged to cooperate in the search for evidence. The standard for a criminal conviction shall be proof beyond a reasonable doubt. Any doubt shall benefit the defendant.[128] The prosecution shall turn over all exculpatory evidence to the defense.[129] However, the defense shall not be required to provide any inculpatory evidence to the prosecution.

144.5 Appeals process shall be an examination of specific errors made by the lower court. Appeals courts shall decide cases only on the basis of law. A court having an appellate jurisdiction shall base its judgement only on whether the application of the law by the lower court is fair and proper.[130]

144.6 The judiciary shall adjourn for recess during the month of August.

Article 145 Appointment and Removal of Judges.

The federal court judges shall be appointed by the President and confirmed by a simple majority vote of the Senate.[131] The state court judges shall be appointed by the Governor of the state and confirmed by a simple majority vote of the Congress of the state. Every appointee shall be judged on the basis of his/her competence for the job and character. The confirmation process shall take no more than thirty working days. If the appointee is neither confirmed nor rejected during this time period, he/she shall be considered confirmed by default. If he/she is rejected, the entire process shall be repeated with a different appointee. To remove a federal judge from the bench shall require a super majority up or down vote in the Senate. To remove a state judge from the bench shall require a super majority up or down vote in the state Congress.

Article 146 Eligibility for Judgeship.

146.1 Every judge shall have a law degree from an accredited university in the republic, shall have passed the state bar exam, and shall have worked as a prosecutor or a defense attorney for no less than five years.

146.2 A person who has served for no less than ten years as a district court judge shall be eligible to be appointed as an appeals court judge. A person who has served for no less than ten years as an appeals court judge, shall be eligible to be appointed as a Supreme Court judge. This clause shall be effective 15 years after the ratification of this constitution.

146.3 A district court judge shall be no less than thirty years of age, an appeals court judge shall be no less than forty years of age, and a Supreme Court judge shall be no less than fifty years of age.

146.4 No convicted felon shall be eligible for a judgeship.

Article 147 Number of Judges.

147.1 Each court shall have three judges. The chief judge in each court shall be the most senior judge. If two or more judges have the same seniority in a federal court, the President shall pick the chief judge for that court. If two or more judges have the same seniority in a state court, the Governor of the state shall pick the chief judge for the court.

147.2 The chief judge of the federal Supreme Court shall be the head of the federal judiciary, and shall be called the chief justice of the republic.

147.3 The chief judge of the state Supreme Court shall be the head of the state judiciary, and shall be called the chief justice of the state.

Article 148 Trying a Minor.

Except as specified in this constitution, the applicable district court shall decide whether a minor shall be tried as an adult or as a juvenile.

Article 149 Trying a Law Enforcement Officer.

Any law enforcement officer involved in the shooting or killing of a legal resident shall be tried in the state district court in a transparent manner. The governor of the state shall appoint a prosecutor with no conflict of interest in the case to prosecute the case.

Article 150 Transfer of Judges.

Every judge, except a Federal Supreme Court judge, shall be randomly transferred at the same salary to an equivalent position in the republic every ten years. The federal government shall pay for the transfer of federal judges, and the receiving state governments shall pay for the transfer of state judges.

Article 151 District Courts.

151.1 A district or a trial court shall be the entry point of the legal process for juvenile, civil and criminal cases; a state district court for violation of the state law or a city law within the state, and a federal district court for violation of a federal law.

151.2 No case shall be filed in more than one district court. A judgement of the first district court may be appealed to in the appeals court in the same state, but shall not be filed or appealed to in any other district court.

Article 152 Associate Judges.

Judges who are not chief judges shall be called associate judges.

Article 153 Legal Jurisdiction.

153.1 The state where the law is violated, shall have the legal jurisdiction on prosecuting the case.[132]

153.2 A fugitive of law shall be transferred to the legal jurisdiction for prosecution of the case.[133]

153.3 A district court shall have original jurisdiction for juvenile, civil, and criminal cases. An appeals court and a supreme court shall have appellate jurisdiction.

Article 154 The Judicial Process.

154.1 The judicial process shall be in the following order: (a). the state district court, the state appeals court in the same state, the state Supreme Court in the same state, the federal Supreme Court, and the Senate or (b). The federal district court, the federal appeals court in the same state, the federal Supreme Court, and the Senate.

154.2 A split decision of a district court may be appealed to in a corresponding appeals court in the same state by the loser within thirty business days of the decision. No case shall be filed or appealed to in more than one appeals court.

154.3 A split decision of an appeals court may be appealed to in a corresponding supreme court by the loser within thirty business days of the decision.

154.4 A split decision of the state Supreme Court may be appealed to in the Federal Supreme Court by the loser within thirty business days of the decision. A split decision of the Federal Supreme Court may be overturned by a super majority up or down vote of the Senate within ninety business days of the decision.

154.5 A unanimous decision of a Court shall be considered final.

154.6 The Federal Supreme Court may choose not to hear an appeal of a case decided upon by a lower court.

154.7 No person shall judge himself or herself in a judicial proceeding.

154.8 An adult legal resident shall be allowed to represent himself/herself legally in a court of law.

154.9 The Federal Supreme Court shall have the power to hear all cases involving constitutional issues.

Article 155 The Salary of a Judge

The salary of a judge shall equal that of a Senator.

Article 156 Criminal Prosecutions.

Every accused legal resident shall have a right to (a) a public defense attorney in a court of law, (b) a speedy, fair, and public trial, (c) confront witnesses against him/her, (d) obtain witnesses in his/her favor, (e) be informed of the nature and cause of accusation, and (f) face his/her accusers.[134]

Article 157 Sentencing.

Sentencing by a court shall take place within thirty business days after the conviction.

Article 158 Trial by Jury.

There shall be no trial by jury.[135]

Article 159 Presumption of Innocence.

A person shall be considered innocent until proven guilty in the court of law.[136]

Article 160. Search and Seizure.

160.1 The right of a legal resident against unreasonable search and seizure shall not be abridged. A warrant to carry out an arrest, search or seizure shall be specific, specifying the place to be searched, and the persons and items to be seized. It shall be signed by an absolute majority of district court judges and shall be based on probable cause.[137]

160.2 A general warrant shall not be allowed.

Article 161 Arrest and Detention.

No person shall be arrested or detained without being informed of the charges against him/her, and without being advised of the right to counsel of an attorney;[138] No person shall be detained for more than two business days after the arrest.[139]

Article 162 Testifying against oneself.

No person shall be compelled to testify against himself or herself.

A confession made under compulsion, torture or threat, or after prolonged arrest or detention shall not be admissible as evidence in the court of law.No person shall be convicted or punished in cases where the only proof against him or her is his or her own confession.[140]

Article 163 Criminal Liability.

No person shall be held criminally liable for an act that was legal when it was committed.[141]

Article 164 Wrongful Conviction.

A person exonerated of a wrongful conviction, shall be fairly compensated by the responsible government.[142]

Article 165 Judicial Limit.

No judiciary shall perform a legislative or an executive function.

Article 166 Judicial Proceedings.

All judicial proceedings shall be documented and published verbatim as a matter of public record.

Article 167 Double Jeopardy.

No person shall be tried or punished twice for the same offense.[143]

Article 168 Criminal Trial Procedural Time Limits.

168.1 Initial hearing / arraignment shall be within two business days of the arrest. If a person is not arraigned within two business days, he/she shall be released. During this arraignment, the defendant shall be informed of the pending legal charges, and shall be informed of his/her right to retain a counsel. If the defendant cannot afford an attorney, the court shall provide him/her with a public attorney. The presiding judges shall decide on setting the bail. The defendant shall be asked to plead guilty or not guilty to the charge.[144] If the plea is guilty, the sentencing date shall be established.

168.2 If the defendant pleads not guilty, a preliminary hearing shall be scheduled within ten business days of the arrest.[145] It shall be a proceeding, after a criminal complaint has been filed by the prosecutor, to determine whether there is enough evidence to require a trial. At such a hearing, the defendant shall have a right to legal counsel. At a preliminary hearing, the judge shall either find that the evidence provides probable cause to believe that the crime was committed, and that the crime was committed by the defendant or else the prosecution shall cease.[146]

168.3 The defendant in a criminal trial shall be indicted within thirty business days of arrest, shall be arraigned (post indictment arraignment) within ten business days of indictment, and shall be tried within seventy business days of indictment.[147] During the second or the post indictment arraignment, the trial date shall be established, if the plea is not guilty. If the plea is guilty, the sentencing date shall be established.

Article 169 Vote in Person.

Every vote cast by a judge in a courtroom shall be cast in person, in order to be valid.

Article 170. Statute of Limitations.

There shall be no statutes of limitations or statutory time limits for filing a law suit.

Article 171 Punishment.

171.1 Punishment, as determined by the due process of law, shall be commensurate with the severity of the crime committed. The severity of the crime shall be determined by its consequences. Third party opinions or recommendations about an alleged criminal shall not be a factor in determination of guilt, innocence or punishment.

171.2 Intent, mental or physical state of an alleged criminal shall not be a factor in determination of guilt, innocence or punishment.

171.3 Goals of punishment shall be retribution and deterrence.

171.4 No punishment shall degrade human dignity.

Article 172 Ignorance of Law.

Ignorance of law shall not be an excuse for violating it.

Article 173 Capital Punishment.

173.1 Capital punishment shall require a unanimous vote among the presiding judges. However, every other penalty, including life imprisonment shall require an absolute majority of votes among them.

173.2 Capital punishment and life imprisonment shall be legal. However, no punishment shall be cruel and unusual (e.g., torture, slow killing, or solitary confinement).[148]

Article 174 Evidence.

174.1 An indictment or a conviction in a court of law shall be based on factual evidence.

174.2 Evidence obtained illegally shall not be admissible in a court of law.

Article 175 Solitary Confinement.

No person shall be sentenced to solitary confinement except for his/her own protection.

Article 176 Prison.

176.1 Each prison shall have adequate lighting and ventilation.

176.2 A prison shall provide each prisoner with adequate clothing, shelter, food, and medical care.

176.3 A prison cell shall be no less than three meters long, three meters wide and three meters high with no more than two prisoners per cell. A sink, a shower, and a toilet shall be provided in each cell for sanitary habitation.

Article 177 Fine.

A fine shall be commensurate with the offense, and shall not be used to increase the government revenues. Unwillingness to pay a fine shall result in incarceration. Inability to pay a fine may result in incarceration or in community service. Unwillingness to perform the assigned community service shall result in incarceration.

Article 178 Free Access to Court System.

Every legal resident shall have a free access to the court system.

Article 179 Incarceration.

179.1 An incarceration shall not cost the prisoner or his/her relatives.

179.2 A defendant shall not be sent to a prison in a civil case.

Article 180. Bail.

The amount of bail shall be determined by the seriousness of the crime, and the likelihood of the defendant not appearing in the court.[149] The passport of the defendant on bail shall be confiscated by the government. Bail may be denied for a very serious crime.

Article 181 Victim of Damages.

A victim of the damages caused by the activities of a public or a private party shall be fairly compensated by the responsible party.[150]

B. Federal District Court.

Article 182 Number of Federal District Courts.

The number of federal district courts allocated to a state shall be directly proportional to the number of legal residents in the state, as determined by the latest census. The average number of federal district courts per state shall be two. However, no state shall have less than one federal district court. The Senate shall determine the number of federal district courts in each state in accordance with this rule, by an absolute majority vote. One federal district court shall be located in each state capital. The location of the others shall be decided by an absolute majority vote of the state Congress.

Article 183 Cases.

All bankruptcy cases, disputes over federal taxes, disputes and claims against the republic, and copyright, trademark, and patent cases shall be tried in a federal district court.

C. Federal Appeals Court.

Article 184 Number of Federal Appeals courts.

 There shall be one federal appeals court in the capital of each state.

D. Federal Supreme Court.

Article 185 Number of Federal Supreme Courts.

There shall be one federal Supreme Court in the capital of the republic.

Article 186 Federal Special Prosecutor.

When requested by an absolute majority vote of the Senate, the Supreme Court, by an absolute majority vote, shall appoint a Federal Special Prosecutor for no more than one year to investigate a federal government official for misconduct while in office. The Senate shall prepare a charter specifying the responsibilities and the authority of the Federal Special Prosecutor along with the annual budget and the purpose of the investigation. In order to avoid a conflict of interest, the Federal Special Prosecutor shall be a lawyer from outside the government. Upon completion of the investigation, the Federal Supreme Court by an absolute majority vote shall dismiss the Federal Special Prosecutor. Hiring and firing of the Federal Special Prosecutor shall not be an executive or a legislative function. The term of the Federal Special Prosecutor may be renewed for one year by an absolute majority vote of: (a) first the Federal Supreme court, and then (b) the Senate. The Federal Special Prosecutor shall be immune from litigation for performing his/her duties. The findings of the Federal Special Prosecutor shall conclude the investigation.

E. State District Court.

Article 187 Number of State District Courts.

There shall be one state district court in each senate district.

Article 188 Cases.

188.1 All intra-state small claims cases shall be tried in a state district court where the defendant lives. All interstate small claims cases shall be tried in a federal district court where the defendant lives.

188.2 No small claim shall exceed ten percent of the median annual household income.

188.3 Probate, family law, and traffic cases shall be tried in an applicable state district court.

F. State Appeals Court.

Article 189 Number of State Appeals Courts.

There shall be one state appeals court in each senate district.

G. Supreme Court.

Article 190. Number of State Supreme Courts.

There shall be one state supreme court in the capital of each state.

Article 191 State Special Prosecutor.

When requested by an absolute majority vote of the state Congress, the State Supreme Court by an absolute majority vote, shall appoint a State Special Prosecutor for no more than one year to investigate a state or a local government official for misconduct while in office. The state Congress shall prepare a charter specifying the responsibilities and the authority of the State Special Prosecutor along with the annual budget and the purpose of the investigation. In order to avoid a conflict of interest, the State Special Prosecutor shall be a lawyer from outside the government. Upon completion of the investigation, the State Supreme Court by an absolute majority vote shall dismiss the State Special Prosecutor. Hiring and firing of the State Special Prosecutor shall not be an executive or a legislative function. The term of the State Special Prosecutor may be renewed for one year by an absolute majority vote of: (a) first the State Supreme Court, and then (b) the state Congress. The State Special Prosecutor shall be immune from litigation for performing his/her duties. The findings of the State Special Prosecutor shall conclude the investigation.

Chapter V: Military, National Guard, State Police, City Police, and Fire Departments

A. General.

Article 192 Service.

192.1 No person shall be drafted more than once for active duty in the Military, the National Guard, the State Police, the City Police or the Fire Departments.

192.2 For a citizen, a general or a dishonorable discharge from any of these services shall require four years of duty as a trash collector as assigned by the President. For a legal immigrant, a general or a dishonorable discharge shall result in a loss of the immigration status followed by an expulsion from the republic.

192.3 If a legal resident dies in the line of duty in any of these services, each of his/her children shall be provided for by the responsible government until he/she is eighteen years of age.

Article 193 Assignments.

193.1 The Military assignments shall be global. The assignments in the National Guard, the State Police, the City Police, and the Fire Departments shall be within the Republic.

193.2 Military, National Guard, the State Police, the City Police, and the Fire Department personnel shall not be quartered in private homes without the consent of the owner.[151]

Article 194 Order of Priority for the draft.

The order of priority for the draft shall be the Military, the City Police, the State Police, the Fire Departments, and the National Guard.

Article 195 Healthcare for Active Duty Members.

Everyone who serves on active duty in the Military, the National Guard, the State Police, the City Police, or the Fire Departments shall be entitled to free healthcare along with his/her family during his/her service. The Federal Government shall pay for the cost of healthcare of the Military personnel. Each State Government shall pay for the healthcare of the State National Guard, plus the State Police, and the Fire Departments that serve the state outside the cities. Each City Government shall pay for the healthcare of the City Police and the Fire Departments that serve the city.

Article 196 Citizen Registering for the Draft.

196.1 Every citizen of the republic shall be required to register for the draft in the Military, the National Guard, the State Police, the City Police, and the Fire Departments within thirty days after his/her eighteenth birthday.

196.2 Every citizen between the ages of eighteen and twenty-six years shall be required to register for. and be eligible for the draft into the active duty Military, the National Guard, the State Police, the City police, and the Fire Departments. The Military shall determine his/her qualifications, including the physical fitness for the active duty military service.

Article 197 Sequence of Draft.

The draft board shall determine the sequence to draft eligible candidates in the Military, the City Police, the State Police, the Fire Departments, and the National Guard. This sequence shall be determined randomly based on birthdays falling on three hundred and sixty-five/six days of a calendar year/leap year respectively. The first birthday drawn shall have priority one, and the last birthday drawn shall have priority three hundred and sixty-five/six. The draft process shall start with priority one and shall proceed in a numerical sequence until it ends with priority three hundred and sixty -five/six

Once all the eligible people at a given priority level are drafted, the draft board shall move on to the next priority level. The draft sequence for each fiscal year shall be determined on the first day of the fiscal year for the eligible candidates between eighteen and twenty-six years of age during the fiscal year, and shall expire at the end of that fiscal year.

Article 198 Draft Dodging/Deferment.

198.1 Draft dodging, draft deferment, absence without authorized leave, and deserting the assigned service shall be illegal.

198.2 No person shall pay or bribe one's way out of a draft.

198.3 No person shall be allowed to enlist in lieu of a draftee.

198.4 If a draftee is unanimously determined to be unfit to serve in the active military duty by three independent military doctors, he/she shall serve in a duty assigned by the President for no less than two years.

Article 199 Paying the Cost.

The federal government shall pay for the cost of the Military. Each state government shall pay for the cost of the National Guard, plus the cost of State Police and the Fire Departments that serve the state outside the cities. Each city government shall pay for the cost of the City Police, and the Fire Department that serve the city.

Article 200. Number of Draftees/Enlistees.

No less than an absolute majority of the Military shall be made up of draftees and first-time enlistees. No less than an absolute majority of the National Guard, the State police, the City Police, and the Fire Departments each shall be made up of draftees.

Article 201 Minimum Draft/Enlistment Period.

201.1 The minimum active duty draft/enlistment period for the Army, and the Marine Corps shall be two years each. For the Navy, the Air Force and the Coast Guard, it shall be four years each.

201.2 The minimum draft period for the National Guard, the State Police, the City Police, and the Fire Departments shall be two years each.

Article 202 Number of National Guard, Fire Fighters and Police Officers.

Unless approved by a super majority vote of a state Congress, there shall be no more than 100 National Guard, no more than 50 fire fighters, and no more than 200 police officers each per 100,000 people in the state as determined by the latest census. The allocation of police officers and fire fighters to each Congressional district shall be directly proportional to its population as determined by the latest census. The National Guard shall work for the Governor of the state.

B. Military.

Article 203 Military Departments.

The military shall be organized into the following departments: the Army, the Air Force, and the Navy. The Coast Guard and the Marine Corps shall be part of the Navy.

Article 204 First Two Years.

The first two years of the active duty military service shall be in a non-commissioned capacity as a private.

Article 205 Immigrant Registering for the Draft.

205.1 Every legal immigrant of the republic shall be required to register for the military draft within thirty days after his/her eighteenth birthday.

205.2 Every legal immigrant between the ages of eighteen and twenty-six years shall be required to register for and be eligible for a draft into the active duty military. The military shall determine his/her qualifications, including the physical fitness for the active duty military service.

Article 206 Conscientious Objector

A citizen who is a conscientious objector to the active duty military service shall be required to serve as a trash collector for four years as assigned by the President. A legal immigrant who is a conscientious objector to the active duty military service shall lose his/her immigrant status permanently, and shall be deported.

Article 207 College Tuition.

The federal government shall pay for four years of college tuition and text books in an accredited public university in the state for every draftee/enlistee, who has served in the military for no less than two years, and has received an honorable discharge.

Article 208 Number of Draftees.

On the first day of every fiscal year, the President, as the Commander-in-chief, shall submit to the federal draft board the total number of draftees required in each Military Department during the fiscal year. The Draft Board shall then start drafting the eligible candidates.

Article 209 Military Constraints.

209.1 Only legal residents shall be allowed to serve in the military. Citizens shall be allowed to serve in any branch of the military. Legal immigrants shall be allowed to serve only in the Army, and the Marine corps.

209.2 Military shall not be used to maintain internal law and order, unless authorized by a super majority vote of the Senate.

209.3 No foreign military base shall be allowed on the soil of the republic.

209.4 The armed forces of the republic shall not fight under the command of a foreign country.

209.5 No less than one percent of the population of the republic as determined by the latest census shall be in the military.

209.6 Annual defense spending shall be no less than five percent of the Gross Domestic Product (GDP) of the republic.

Article 210 Eligibility for Citizenship.

A legal immigrant between eighteen and twenty-six years of age shall have to serve on active duty in the military for no less than two years with an honorable discharge in order to be eligible for citizenship.

Article 211 Enlisting in the Military.

Any physically fit legal resident between the ages of eighteen and twenty-six years may volunteer to serve for no less than two years of active duty in the military. This shall be legally equivalent to the service rendered by a draftee, if accompanied by an honorable discharge.

Article 212 Command of an Activity.

No military commander shall have the command of an activity or an organization for more than three years.

Article 213 Uniform Code of Military Justice.

Uniform code of military justice as passed by an absolute majority vote of the Senate and signed by the President shall govern the armed forces.

Article 214 Military Courts.

Each military court shall have three judges, a prosecutor and a defense attorney, who shall be commissioned officers on active duty in different military departments. The chief judge in each court shall be the highest-ranking officer in the court. If two or more judges have the same rank, the most senior officer shall be the chief judge. If two or more judges with same rank have the same seniority, the President shall choose the chief judge. The jurisdiction of each departmental court shall be limited to intra-departmental legal issues. There shall be an overarching court in the capital of the republic to deal with inter-departmental legal issues. No military court shall be located on a military base of its own department. Each court decision shall be independent and final.

Article 215 Prisoners of War.

Treatment of Prisoners of War (POWs) shall be subject to the Geneva Convention.

C. National Guard, State Police, City Police, and Fire Departments.

Article 216 Service Constraints.

Only citizens shall be drafted into the National Guard, the State Police, the City Police, or the Fire Departments to serve within the republic. There shall be no enlistments into these services.

Article 217 Qualification Criteria.

Each State Governor shall determine the qualification criteria for the draftees in the National Guard, plus the draftees in the State Police, and the Fire Departments that will serve in the state outside the cities. Each City Mayor shall determine the qualification criteria for the draftees in the City Police and the Fire Departments that will serve in the city.

Article 218 Tuition and Text Books.

Each State Government shall pay for four years of tuition and text books in an accredited public university in the state for every draftee who has served in the National Guard in the state, plus every draftee who has served in the State Police or the Fire Departments in the state outside the cities with an honorable discharge. Each City Government shall pay for four years of tuition and text books in an accredited public university in the state for every draftee who has served the city in the City Police or the Fire Departments with an honorable discharge.

Article 219 Number of Draftees Required.

On the first day of every fiscal year, each State Governor shall submit to the federal draft board the number of draftees required for the National Guard within his/her state, plus the number of draftees required for the State Police, and the Fire Departments within his/her state outside the cities for the fiscal year. On the first day of every fiscal year, each City Mayor shall submit to the federal draft board the number of draftees required for the City Police and the Fire Departments within his/her city for the fiscal year. The federal draft board, with the concurrence of the President, shall draft the eligible candidates to meet the needs of each state and city after the needs of the Military have been met.

Chapter VI: Education

Article 220 Medium of Instruction.

English shall be the medium of instruction in every educational institution.

Article 221 K-12 Education.

221.1 The federal government with the help of state and local governments shall be responsible for providing free Kindergarten through 12th grade (K-12) public education to all legal residents.[152]

221.2 K-12 education, provided by public schools or government accredited private schools, shall be mandatory for all legal residents. Public schools shall be financed by federal, state and local income and sales taxes.

221.3 The federal government shall be responsible for paying half of the K-12 public educational expenses in each state. The matching half shall be paid for by the state government. The federal and state funding per student shall be uniform throughout the republic. Non-educational expenses shall be paid for by the state.

221.4 The federal government shall set uniform educational standards and curricula for all the K-12 students in the republic.[153] The state and local governments shall implement and administer them.

221.5 Federal education funds allocated to a state shall be directly proportional to the number of students attending the K-12 public educational institutions in the state.

221.6 Public funds shall not be used to finance private education.

221.7 In addition to English, every student shall be required to learn a foreign language from grade six through grade twelve.

Article 222 Home Schooling.

Home schooling shall be illegal.[154]

Article 223 Licensing and Accreditation.

Each state government shall be responsible for licensing and accrediting the public educational institutions operating within the state.   The federal government shall license and accredit all the private educational institutions in the republic. Only a diploma or a degree from an accredited educational institution shall be recognized.

Article 224 College Education.

224.1 The annual cost of tuition to a legal resident student in a public university shall not exceed five percent of the median annual household income.

224.2 State and local income and sales taxes shall finance the public university education within the state. Each state government shall set, implement, and administer uniform educational standards and curricula for all the public university students within the State.

224.3 A public university or an institution of higher learning in a state shall admit no less than eighty percent of its undergraduate students from the high school graduates within the state on a competitive basis.

224.4 No more than five percent of the total number of students in a public university or an institution of higher learning shall be on a student visa.

224.5 Admission to and scholarship for an institution of higher learning shall be based purely on academic merit.

Article 225 Board Examination.

At the end of the high school and after four years of college, there shall be a state administered board examination that every student shall be required to pass in order to graduate. The passing grade shall be seventy percent of the maximum possible. Each student shall be assigned an identification number for the examination, and shall not be allowed to use his/her name.

Glossary

The following definitions and meanings apply to this constitution.

To abridge: To make shorter; to shorten in duration; to lessen; to diminish; to curtail.[155]

To absolve: To free from a penalty; to pardon.[156]

To acquit: To set free, release or discharge from an obligation, duty, liability, burden, or from an accusation or charge.[157]

A.D.: Anno Domini [Latin: in the year of [our] Lord Jesus Christ]; In the year of the Christian era; as, A.D. 1887.[158]

To administer: To manage or supervise the conduct, performance or execution of.[159]

An adult is a person no less than eighteen years of age.

Affectation: An attempt to assume or exhibit what is not natural or real; false display; artificial show.[160]

Appeal: In law, an appeal is the process in which cases are reviewed, where parties request a formal change to an official decision. Appeals function both as a process for error correction as well as a process of clarifying and interpreting law.[161]

Appellate Court: In the United States, both state and federal appellate courts are usually restricted to examining whether the lower court made the correct legal determinations, rather than hearing direct evidence and determining what the facts of the case were. Furthermore, U.S. appellate courts are usually restricted to hearing appeals based on matters that were originally brought up before the trial court. Hence, such an appellate court will not consider an appellant's argument if it is based on a theory that is raised for the first time in the appeal.

In most U.S. states, and in U.S. federal courts, parties before the court are allowed one appeal as of right. This means that a party who is unsatisfied with the outcome of a trial may bring an appeal to contest that outcome. However, appeals may be costly, and the appellate court must find an error on the part of the court below that justifies upsetting the verdict. Therefore, only a small proportion of trial court decisions result in appeals. Some appellate courts, particularly supreme courts, have the power of discretionary review, meaning that they can decide whether they will hear an appeal brought in a particular case.[162]

Appellate jurisdiction: Appellate jurisdiction is the power of a higher court to review decisions and change outcomes of decisions of lower courts.[163]

Appropriate: To set apart for, or assign to, a particular person or use, in exclusion of all others; -- with to or for; as, a spot of ground is appropriated for a garden; to appropriate money for the increase of the navy.[164]

Appropriation: The act of setting apart or assigning to a particular use or person, or of taking to one's self, in exclusion of all others; application to a special use or purpose, as of a piece of ground for a park, or of money to carry out some object.[165]

Arbitration: is a way to resolve disputes outside the courts. It can be either voluntary or mandatory (although mandatory arbitration can only come from a statute or from a contract that one party imposes on the other, in which the parties agree to hold all existing or future disputes to arbitration, without necessarily knowing, specifically, what disputes will ever occur) and can be either binding or non-binding.[166]

To arraign: To call or set as a prisoner at the bar of a court to answer to the matter charged in an indictment or complaint.[167]

Arraignment: is a formal reading of a criminal charging document in the presence of the defendant. In response to arraignment, the defendant is expected to enter a plea.[168]

Assault: A violent onset or attack with physical means, as blows, weapons, etc.; an onslaught.[169]

B.C.: Before Christ, an epoch used in dating years prior to the estimated birth of Jesus in the Julian and Gregorian calendars.[170]

Bequest: 1. the act of bequeathing or leaving by will; as, a bequest of property by A to B. 2. That which is left by will, esp. personal property; a legacy; also, a gift.[171]

Bibliography: A history or description of books and manuscripts, with notices of the different editions, the times when they were printed, etc.[172]

Bill: A bill is proposed legislation under consideration by a legislature. A bill does not become law until it is passed by the legislature and, in most cases, approved by the executive. Once a bill has been enacted into law, it is called an *act of the legislature*, or a *statute*.[173]

Certiorari: [So named from the emphatic word certiorari in the Latin form of the writ, which read certiorar volumus we wish to be certified.] A writ issuing out of chancery, or a superior court, to call up the records of an inferior court, or remove a cause there depending, in order that the party may have more sure and speedy justice, or that errors and irregularities may be corrected. It is obtained upon complaint of a party that he has not received justice, or cannot have an impartial trial in the inferior court.[174]

Chain Migration: The term refers to the process of foreign nationals immigrating to a new country under laws permitting their reunification with family members already living in the destination country.[175]

Checks and balances: is the principle that each of the Branches has the power to limit or check the other two and this creates a balance between the three separate powers of the state, this principle induces that the ambitions of one branch prevent that one of the other branches become supreme, and thus be eternally confronting each other and in that process leaving the people free from government abuses. Checks and Balances are designed to maintain the system of separation of powers keeping each branch in its place.[176]

Citizen: A person, native or naturalized, of either sex, who owes allegiance to a government, and is entitled to reciprocal protection from it.[177]

Civil law: is non-criminal law. The law relating to civil wrongs and quasi-contracts is part of the civil law, as is law of property (other than property-related crimes, such as theft or vandalism). The rights and duties of persons amongst themselves is the primary concern of civil law. It is often suggested that civil proceedings are taken for the purpose of obtaining compensation for injury, and may thus be distinguished from criminal proceedings, whose purpose is to inflict punishment.[178]

Cloture: Cloture is a motion or process in parliamentary procedure aimed at bringing debate to a quick end.[179]

Codification: The act or process of codifying or reducing laws to a code.[180]

Collusion: A secret agreement and cooperation for a fraudulent or deceitful purpose; a playing into each other's hands; deceit; fraud; cunning.[181]

Commensurate: Equal in measure or extent; proportionate.[182]

Constitution: The fundamental, organic law or principles of government of men, embodied in written documents, or implied in the institutions and usages of the country or society; also, a written instrument embodying such organic law, and laying down fundamental rules and principles for the conduct of affairs.[183]

Convertible: Capable of being exchanged or interchanged; reciprocal; interchangeable.[184]

Conviction: A judgment of condemnation entered by a court having jurisdiction; the act or process of finding guilty, or the state of being found guilty of any crime by a legal tribunal.[185]

Court order: A court order is an official proclamation by a judge (or panel of judges) that defines the legal relationships between the parties to a hearing, a trial, an appeal or other court proceedings. Such ruling requires or authorizes the carrying out of certain steps by one or more parties to a case. An order can be as simple as setting a date for trial.[186]

Crime: A crime is an unlawful act harmful not only to some individual but also to a community, society or the state ("a public wrong"). Such acts are forbidden and punishable by law. While every crime violates the law, not every violation of the law counts as a crime.[187]

Criminal law: The law which relates to crimes.[188]

Democracy: Government by popular representation; a form of government in which the supreme power is retained by the people, but is indirectly exercised through a system of representation and delegated authority periodically renewed; a constitutional representative government.[189]

District Court: The United States district courts are the general trial courts of the United States federal court system. Both civil and criminal cases are filed in the district court, which is a court of law, equity, and admiralty. There is a United States bankruptcy court associated with each United States district court. There are 89 districts in the 50 states, with a total of 94 districts including territories.[190]

Due process: Due process is the legal requirement that the state must respect all legal rights that are owed to a person.[191]

Duty: Duty is tax on certain items purchased abroad.[192]

Economic refugee: is an individual who seeks refugee status in another country solely for economic reasons.

Eminent Domain: Eminent domain (United States, the Philippines), compulsory purchase (United Kingdom, New Zealand, Ireland), resumption (Hong Kong), resumption/compulsory acquisition (Australia), or expropriation (France, Mexico, South Africa, Canada, Brazil, Portugal, Spain) is the power of a state or a national government to take private property for public use.[193]

Equality: means equality of rights before the law.

etc. = et cētera (L. et and + caetera other things) = Others of the like kind; and the rest; and so on.[194]

Excise: An excise or excise tax is any duty on manufactured goods which is levied at the moment of manufacture, rather than at sale.[195]

To exculpate: To clear from alleged fault or guilt; to prove to be guiltless; to relieve of blame; to acquit.[196]

Exculpatory evidence: favorable to the defendant in a criminal trial that exonerates or tends to exonerate the defendant of guilt. It is the opposite of inculpatory evidence, which tends to present guilt.[197]

Excursion: An expedition; a journey chiefly for recreation, a pleasure trip.[198]

e.g. = exempli gratia (in Latin) = for example.

To exonerate: To relieve, in a moral sense, as of a charge, obligation, or load of blame resting on one.[199]

Ex parte: is a Latin legal term meaning "from (by or for) [the/a] party." An *ex parte* decision is one decided by a judge without requiring all of the parties to the controversy to be present. Ex *parte* can also mean a legal proceeding brought by one person in the absence of and without representation or notification of other parties.[200]

Family: The group comprising a husband and wife and their dependent children, constituting a fundamental unit in the organization of society.[201]

Felony: In the United States, where the felony/misdemeanor distinction is still widely applied, the federal government defines a felony as a crime punishable by death or imprisonment in excess of one year. If punishable by exactly one year or less, it is classified as a misdemeanor.[202]

Filibuster: A filibuster in the United States Senate is a dilatory or obstructive tactic used in the United States Senate to prevent a measure from being brought to a vote.[203]

Habeas Corpus: [Latin. you may have the body.] (Law) A writ having for its object to bring a party before a court or judge; especially, one to inquire into the cause of a person's imprisonment or detention by another, with the view to protect the right to personal liberty; also, one to bring a prisoner into court to testify in a pending trial.[204]

Hammurabi: means the kinsman (blood relation) is a healer. (Ammu= paternal kinsman, Rāpi= healer).[205]

To harass: To fatigue; to tire with repeated and exhausting efforts; to cause to endure excessive burdens or anxieties.[206]

Household: A household consists of one or more people who reside in the same dwelling and also share meals or living accommodation, and may consist of a single family or some other grouping of people.[207]

Ibidem: adv. [Latin.] In the same place; -- abbreviated ibid. or ib.[208]

i.e.: Abbreviation of Latin id est, that is.[209]

Illegal: Not according to, or authorized by, law; contrary to, or in violation of, human law; unlawful.[210]

Immigrant: One who immigrates; one who comes to a country for the purpose of permanent residence.[211]

Impeachment: A calling to account; arraignment; especially, of a public officer for maladministration.[212]

Incest: is human sexual activity between family members or close relatives. This typically includes sexual activity between people in consanguinity (blood relations), and sometimes those related by affinity (marriage or stepfamily), adoption, clan, or lineage.[213]

To inculpate: (Latin inculpare= to blame) To blame; to impute guilt to; to accuse; to involve or implicate in guilt.[214]

Inculpatory: Imputing blame; criminatory; compromising; implicating.[215]

Indenture: To bind by indentures or written contract; as, to indenture an apprentice; as, to indent a young man to a shoemaker; to indent a servant.[216]

To indict: To charge with a crime, in due form of law; as, to indict a man for arson.[217]

To infringe: [Latin. infringere; pref. in- in + frangere to break] 1. To break; to violate; to transgress; to neglect to fulfill or obey; as, to infringe a law or contract.[218]

Initiative: An initiative is a means through which any citizen or organization may gather a predetermined number of signatures to qualify a measure to be placed on a ballot, and to be voted upon in a future election.[219]

Injunction: A writ or process, granted by a court of equity, and, in some cases, under statutes, by a court of law, whereby a party is required to do or to refrain from doing certain acts, according to the exigency of the writ.[220]

Insider trading: is the trading of a public company's stock or other securities (such as bonds or stock options) by individuals with access to nonpublic information about the company.[221]

Intestate: [Latin. intestatus; pref. in- not + testatus, p. p. of testari to make a will] without having made a valid will; without a will; as, to die intestate.[222]

Involuntary: Not proceeding from choice; done unwillingly; reluctant; compulsory; as, involuntary submission.[223]

Judicial review: is a process under which executive and (in some countries) legislative actions are subject to review by the judiciary. A court with judicial review power may invalidate laws and decisions that are incompatible with a higher authority; an executive decision may be invalidated for being unlawful or a statute may be invalidated for violating the terms of a written constitution.[224]

Jurisdiction: Jurisdiction (from the Latin *ius, iuris* meaning "law" and *dicere* meaning "to speak") is the practical authority granted to a legal body to administer justice within a defined field of responsibility.[225]

Justice: The rendering to everyone his due or right; just treatment; merited reward or punishment; equity; fairness; impartiality.[226]

Law: An organic rule, as a constitution or charter, establishing and defining the conditions of the existence of a state or other organized community. Any edict, decree, order, ordinance, statute, resolution, judicial, decision, usage, etc., or recognized, and enforced, by the controlling authority.[227]

Legal resident: is either a citizen or a legal immigrant.

Liberty: means economic, political, religious, and social freedom, freedom of movement and travel, freedom of expression and press, freedom of peaceful assembly, petition, and demonstration, without retaliation from the government.

To litigate: To make the subject of a lawsuit; to contest in law; to carry on a suit by judicial process.[228]

Majority: a. Absolute: An absolute majority means more than fifty percent of all electors or the total membership, not just those who voted. b. Simple: A simple majority means more than fifty percent of the votes cast. c. Super: A super majority means no less than two third of all electors or the total membership, not just those who voted.[229]

Mandamus: (/ˈmænˈdeɪməs/; Latin "we command") is a judicial remedy in the form of an order from a court to any government, subordinate court, corporation, or public authority, to do (or forbear from doing) some specific act which that body is obliged under law to do (or refrain from doing), and which is in the nature of public duty, and in certain cases one of a statutory duty.[230]

Markup: The process by which legislative committees and subcommittees debate, amend, and rewrite proposed legislation.[231]

Martial law: is the imposition of direct military control of normal civilian functions of government, especially in response to a temporary emergency such as invasion or major disaster, or in an occupied territory.[232]

Mental abuse: is a form of abuse characterized by a person subjecting another to a behavior that may result in psychological trauma.

Minor: is a person less than eighteen years of age.

Money laundering: is the process of transforming the profits of crime and corruption into ostensibly "legitimate" assets.[233]

Nepotism: is favor granted to relatives in various fields, including business, politics, entertainment, sports, religion and other activities. The term originated with the assignment of nephews to important positions by Catholic pope and bishops. The term comes from the Italian word *nepotism,* which is based on the Latin word *nepos* meaning 'nephew'.[234]

Obstruction of justice: The crime of obstruction of justice, in United States jurisdictions, refers to the crime of obstructing prosecutors or other (usually government) officials. Common law jurisdictions other than the United States tend to use the wider offense of perverting the course of justice.[235]

Original jurisdiction: The original jurisdiction of a court is the power to hear a case for the first time, as opposed to appellate jurisdiction, when a higher court has the power to review a lower court's decision.[236]

Pardon: (Law) a release, by a sovereign, or officer having jurisdiction, from the penalties of an offense, being distinguished from amnesty, which is a general obliteration and canceling of a particular line of past offenses.[237]

Party discipline: is the ability of a parliamentary group of a political party to get its members to support the policies of their party leadership.[238]

Perjury: is the intentional act of swearing a false oath or of falsifying an affirmation to tell the truth, whether spoken or in writing, concerning matters material to an official proceeding.[239]

Pernicious: [Latin. perniciosus, from pernicies destruction, from pernecare to kill or slay outright; per + necare to kill, slay.] Having the quality of injuring or killing; destructive; very mischievous; baleful; malicious; wicked.[240]

Physical abuse: is any intentional act causing injury or trauma to another person by way of bodily contact.

Plead: To argue in support of a claim, or in defense against the claim of another; to urge reasons for or against a thing; to attempt to persuade one by argument or supplication; to speak by way of persuasion; as, to plead for the life of a criminal; to plead with a judge or with a father.[241]

Political refugee: is a person, who has fled from the homeland because of political persecution.

Posse Comitatus: [Latin. posse to be able, to have power + comitatus a county]. The power of the county, or the citizens who may be summoned by the sheriff to assist the authorities in suppressing a riot, or executing any legal precept which is forcibly opposed.[242]

Preamble: [Latin. praeambulus = walking before]. An introductory portion; an introduction or preface, as to a book, document, etc.; specifically, the introductory part of a statute, which states the reasons and intent of the law.[243]

Precedent: A judicial decision which serves as a rule for future determinations in similar or analogous cases; an authority to be followed in courts of justice; forms of proceeding to be followed in similar cases.[244]

Presumption: The act of presuming, or believing upon probable evidence; the act of assuming or taking for granted; belief upon incomplete proof.[245]

Price gouging: is defined as raising the prices of goods, services or commodities to a level much higher than is considered fair or reasonable.

Prisoner of War (POW): is a person, whether combatant or non-combatant, who is held in custody by a belligerent power during or immediately after an armed conflict.[246]

Probable cause: is a reasonable amount of suspicion, supported by circumstances sufficiently strong to justify a prudent and cautious person's belief that certain facts are probably true.[247]

Probate: Official proof; especially, the proof before a competent officer or tribunal that an instrument offered, purporting to be the last will and testament of a person deceased, is indeed his lawful act; the copy of a will proved, under the seal of the Court of Probate, delivered to the executors with a certificate of its having been proved.[248]

Provision: That which is stipulated in advance; a condition; a previous agreement; a proviso; as, the provisions of a contract; the statute has many provisions.[249]

Ratify: to make valid; to confirm; to establish; to settle; as, to ratify an agreement,[250]

Referendum: A referendum (plural: referendums or referenda) is a direct vote in which an entire electorate is invited to vote on a particular proposal. This may result in the adoption of a new law.[251]

Refugee: One who, in times of persecution or political commotion, flees to a foreign power or country for safety.[252]

To regulate: To adjust by rule, method, or established mode; to direct by rule or restriction; to subject to governing principles or laws.[253]

Religious refugee: is a person, who is a refugee because of his/her religion.

Reprieve: A temporary suspension of the execution of a sentence, especially of a sentence of death.[254]

Republic: is a constitutional form of government.

Secularity: Supreme attention to the things of the present life; worldliness.[255]

Sedition: The raising of commotion in a state, not amounting to insurrection; conduct tending to treason, but without an overt act; excitement of discontent against the government, or of resistance to lawful authority.[256]

The separation of powers: is a model for the governance of a state. Under this model, a state's government is divided into branches, each with separate and independent powers and areas of responsibility so that the powers of one branch are not in conflict with the powers associated with the other branches. The typical division is into three branches: a legislature, an executive, and a judiciary, which is the *trias politica* model.[257]

Serf: is one bound to work on a certain estate, and thus attached to the soil, and sold with it into the service of whoever purchases the land.[258]

Sexual: Of or pertaining to sex, or the sexes.[259]

Sic: The Latin adverb *sic* ("thus", "just as"; in full: *sic erat scriptum*, "thus was it written").[260]

Slave: A person who is held in bondage to another; one who is wholly subject to the will of another; one who has no freedom of action, but whose person and services are wholly under the control of another.[261]

Snap election: is an election called earlier than expected. Generally it refers to an election in a parliamentary system called when not required (either by law or convention), usually to capitalize on a unique electoral opportunity or to decide a pressing issue.[262]

Sovereign: Supreme or highest in power; superior to all others.[263]

Sovereignty: Independence.[264]

Stare decisis: The principle by which judges are bound to precedents is known as stare decisis.[265]

Statute: An act of the legislature of a state or country, declaring, commanding, or prohibiting something; a positive law; the written will of the legislature expressed with all the requisite forms of legislation.[266]

Statute of limitations: Statutes of limitations are laws passed by legislative bodies in common law systems to set the maximum time after an event within which legal proceedings may be initiated.[267]

Subpoena: (Latin. sub under + poena punishment.) (Law) A writ commanding the attendance in court, as a witness, of the person on whom it is served, under a penalty.[268]

Suffrage: The formal expression of an opinion; assent; vote.[269]

Supreme Court: A supreme court is the highest court within the hierarchy of courts in many legal jurisdictions. Other descriptions for such courts include court of last resort, apex court, and highest (or final) court of appeal. Broadly speaking, the decisions of a supreme court are not subject to further review by any other court. Supreme courts typically function primarily as appellate courts, hearing appeals from decisions of lower trial courts, or from intermediate-level appellate courts.[270]

Tariff: A tariff is a tax on imports or exports between sovereign states.[271]

Terrorism: is the use of violence and intimidation in the pursuit of political, religious or ideological aims.

Testate: (Law) One who leaves a valid will at death; a testate person.[272]

Tort: A tort, in common law jurisdictions, is a civil wrong that causes a claimant to suffer loss or harm resulting in legal liability for the person who commits the tortious act.[273]

Torture: Severe pain inflicted judicially, either as punishment for a crime, or for the purpose of extorting a confession from an accused person.[274]

Treason: The offense of attempting to overthrow the government of the state to which the offender owes allegiance, or of betraying the state into the hands of a foreign power; disloyalty; treachery.[275]

Unfunded liability: is the gap between the amount of promised benefits and the resources set aside to pay for them.[276]

Usury: Interest in excess of a legal rate charged to a borrower for the use of money.[277]

Victimless crime: is an illegal act that typically either directly involves only the perpetrator, or occurs between consenting adults; because it is consensual in nature, there is arguably no true victim.[278]

Vindicate: To support or maintain as true or correct, against denial, censure, or objections; to defend; to justify; to liberate; to set free.[279]

Warrant: A warrant is generally an order that serves as a specific type of authorization, that is, a writ issued by a competent officer, usually a judge or magistrate, which permits an otherwise illegal act that would violate individual rights and affords the person executing the writ protection from damages if the act is performed. A warrant is usually issued by a court and is directed to a sheriff, a constable, or a police officer.[280]

Witness tampering: is the act of attempting to alter or prevent the testimony of witnesses within criminal or civil proceedings.[281]

Writ: In common law, a writ is a formal written order issued by a body with administrative or judicial jurisdiction; in modern usage, this body is generally a court. Warrants, prerogative writs, and subpoenas are common types of writ, but many forms exist and have existed.[282]

Bibliography

"About the Supreme Court," *United States Courts*, Accessed August 26, 2016, http://www.uscourts.gov/about-federal-courts/educational-resources/about-educational-outreach/activity-resources/about

"America's Founding Documents," *National Archives*. (Last reviewed: September 25, 2018). https://www.archives.gov/founding-docs/constitution-q-and-a

Aristotle, *Politics A Treatise on Government*, Translated by William Ellis, (Produced by Eric Eldred, and David Widger, Release Date: June 5, 2009 [E Book # 6962], Last updated: January 12, 2013). http://www.gutenberg.org/files/6762/6762-h/6762-h.htm#link2HCH0019

Arnheim, Michael. *U.S. Constitution for dummies*. Hoboken, New Jersey: John Wiley and Sons, Inc., 2018.

The Cabinet Manual, 1st Edition, October 2011, https://assets.publishing.service.gov.uk/government/uploads/system/uploads/attachment_data/file/60641/cabinet-manual.pdf

Centers for Medicare and Medicaid Services, National Health Expenditure (NHE) Fact Sheet, Accessed February 6, 2019. https://www.cms.gov/research-statistics-data-and-systems/statistics-trends-and-reports/nationalhealthexpenddata/nhe-fact-sheet.html

Congressional Record Volume 146, Number 142 (Wednesday, November 1, 2000), Senate, page S11495. https://www.gpo.gov/fdsys/pkg/CREC-2000-11-01/html/CREC-2000-11-01-pt1-PgS11494-4.htm,

The Constitution of the United States of America, Washington, DC: Superintendent of Documents, Government Printing Office, 2007.

https://www.gpo.gov/fdsys/pkg/CDOC-110hdoc50/pdf/CDOC-110hdoc50.pdf

The French Legal System, Edited by Ministry of Justice, 2012. Accessed February 25, 2019. http://www.justice.gouv.fr/art_pix/french_legal_system.pdf

Handy, Kevin, Reigel, Lisa, Hagerson, John, and the Project Gutenberg Online Distributed Proofreading Team, *The Constitution of the United States of America: Analysis and Interpretation*, ed. Edward Corwin, Release Date: June 20, 2006, [eBook #18637]. http://www.gutenberg.org/cache/epub/18637/pg18637.txt

Harper, Tim. *The Complete Idiot's Guide to the U.S. Constitution.* New York: Alpha, 2007.

"How can I stand in an election?," *U.K. Parliament Home Page*, Accessed September 6, 2016. http://www.parliament.uk/get-involved/elections/standing/

"Hung Parliament," *U.K. Parliament Homepage*, Accessed November 24, 2018. https://www.parliament.uk/about/how/elections-and-voting/general/hung-parliament/

Japan, *The Constitution of Japan, 1946*, Posting date: July 26, 2008 (E Book # 612), Japan: 1946. http://www.gutenberg.org/cache/epub/612/pg612.txt

"Judicial Review", *Courts and Tribunals Judiciary*, Accessed November 25, 2018. https://www.judiciary.uk/you-and-the-judiciary/judicial-review/

Machiavelli, Niccolò, *The Art of War*, Translated by Henry Neville, Wikisource contributors, "The Art of War (Machiavelli)/Book 1," Accessed January 13, 2019.

Wikisource https://en.wikisource.org/w/index.php?title=The_Art_of_War_(Machiavelli)/Book_1&oldid=5920295

Machiavelli, Niccolò, *Discourses on the first Decade of Titus Livius*, Translated by Ninian Thomson, (Produced by Ted Garvin, Jayam Subramanian and PG distributed Proofreaders, Release Date: January 25, 2004 [E Book # 10827]). http://www.gutenberg.org/cache/epub/10827/pg10827

Machiavelli, Niccolò, *The Prince,* Translated by W.K. Marriott, (Produced by John Bickers, David Widger and others, Release Date: February 11, 2006 [E Book # 1232], Last updated: July 11, 2016). http://www.gutenberg.org/files/1232/1232-h/1232-h.htm#link2HCH0012

Monk, Linda. *The words we live by: your annotated guide .to the constitution.* New York: Hyperion, 2003.

"Office and Role of Speaker," *U.K. Parliament Home Page*, Accessed September 12, 2016. http://www.parliament.uk/business/commons/the-Speaker/the-role-of-the-Speaker/role-of-the-Speaker/

Office of the United States Attorneys, Initial Hearing / Arraignment, Accessed February 9, 2019. https://www.justice.gov/usao/justice-101/initial-hearing

Office of the United States Attorneys, Preliminary Hearing. Accessed February 9, 2019. https://www.justice.gov/usao/justice-101/preliminary-hearing

"Parliamentary sovereignty," *U.K. Parliament Home Page*, Accessed September 1, 2016. http://www.parliament.uk/about/how/sovereignty/

"Passage of a Bill," *U.K. Parliament Home Page*, Accessed September 15, 2016.
http://www.parliament.uk/about/how/laws/passage-bill/

Ritchie, Donald. *Our Constitution*. Oxford; New York: Oxford University Press, 2006.

"The Supreme Court of the United States and the Federal Judiciary." *Federal Judicial Center*, August 26, 2016.
http://www.fjc.gov/history/home.nsf/page/courts_supreme.html

Twain, Mark. *Roughing It* 1880. Release Date: August 18, 2006 [EBook #3177]
Last Updated: February 24, 2018,
http://www.gutenberg.org/files/3177/3177-0.txt

"U.S. Electoral College," *National Archives and Records Administration*, Accessed November 27, 2016.
https://www.archives.gov/federal-register/electoral-college/about.html

United States Senate, Glossary Term, Markup,
https://www.senate.gov/reference/glossary_term/markup.htm

Washington, George, *Washington's Farewell Address to the People of the United States*, Washington, DC: Superintendent of Documents, Government Printing Office, 2000.
https://www.gpo.gov/fdsys/pkg/GPO-CDOC-106sdoc21/pdf/GPO-CDOC-106sdoc21.pdf

Acknowledgements

I thank my wife, Beverly, for editing this book, and for providing many valuable comments. I also thank her for formatting and organizing the manuscript to turn it into the final product. I thank my daughter, Nina, for providing grammatical expertise.

Index

Notes

---

[1] Niccolò Machiavelli, *The Prince,* trans. W.K. Marriott, (Produced by John Bickers, David Widger and others, Release Date: February 11, 2006 [E Book # 1232], Last updated: July 11, 2016), Chapter XII, http://www.gutenberg.org/files/1232/1232-h/1232-h.htm#link2HCH0012

[2] Niccolò Machiavelli, *Discourses on the First Decade of Titus Livius*, trans. Ninian Thomson, (Produced by Ted Garvin, Jayam Subramanian and PG distributed Proofreaders, Release Date: January 25, 2004 [E Book # 10827]), Book I, Chapter III, http://www.gutenberg.org/cache/epub/10827/pg10827

[3] Niccolò Machiavelli, *The Art of War*, Part 1, trans. Henry Neville, Wikisource contributors, "The Art of War (Machiavelli)/Book 1," *Wikisource* https://en.wikisource.org/w/index.php?title=The_Art_of_War_(Machiavelli)/Book_1&oldid=5920295 (accessed January 13, 2019).

[4] Aristotle, *Politics A Treatise on Government*, trans. William Ellis, (Produced by Eric Eldred, and David Widger, Release Date: June 5, 2009 [E Book # 6962], Last updated: January 12, 2013), Book II, Chapter VI, http://www.gutenberg.org/files/6762/6762-h/6762-h.htm#link2HCH0019

[5] Aristotle, *Politics A Treatise on Government*, trans. William Ellis, (Produced by Eric Eldred, and David Widger, Release Date: June 5, 2009 [E Book # 6962], Last updated: January 12, 2013), Book V, Chapter VIII, http://www.gutenberg.org/files/6762/6762-h/6762-h.htm#link2HCH0019

[6] Aristotle, *Politics A Treatise on Government*, trans. William Ellis, (Produced by Eric Eldred, and David Widger, Release Date: June 5, 2009 [E Book # 6962], Last updated: January 12, 2013), Book VI,

Chapter IV, http://www.gutenberg.org/files/6762/6762-h/6762-h.htm#link2HCH0019

[7] Aristotle, *Politics A Treatise on Government*, trans. William Ellis, (Produced by Eric Eldred, and David Widger, Release Date: June 5, 2009 [E Book # 6962], Last updated: January 12, 2013), Book III, Chapter X, http://www.gutenberg.org/files/6762/6762-h/6762-h.htm#link2HCH0019

[8] Wikipedia contributors, "Hammurabi," *Wikipedia, The Free Encyclopedia,* https://en.wikipedia.org/w/index.php?title=Hammurabi&oldid=733993885 (accessed August 13, 2016).

[9] Where B.C. is not specified for a given year, A.D. is implied.

[10] George Washington, *Washington's Farewell Address to the People of the United states*, (Washington, DC: Superintendent of Documents, Government Printing Office, 2000), 16, PDF e Book, https://www.gpo.gov/fdsys/pkg/GPO-CDOC-106sdoc21/pdf/GPO-CDOC-106sdoc21.pdf

[11] *The Constitution of the United States of America*, Presented by Mr. Brady of Pennsylvania, July 25, 2007, (Washington, DC: Superintendent of Documents, Government Printing Office, 2007), 20 (Amendment XIX), PDF e Book, https://www.gpo.gov/fdsys/pkg/CDOC-110hdoc50/pdf/CDOC-110hdoc50.pdf

[12] *The Constitution of the United States of America*, Presented by Mr. Brady of Pennsylvania, July 25, 2007, (Washington, DC: Superintendent of Documents, Government Printing Office, 2007), 19 (Amendment XVII), PDF e Book, https://www.gpo.gov/fdsys/pkg/CDOC-110hdoc50/pdf/CDOC-110hdoc50.pdf

13 *The Constitution of the United States of America*, Presented by Mr. Brady of Pennsylvania, July 25, 2007, (Washington, DC: Superintendent of Documents, Government Printing Office, 2007), 2 (Article I, Section 3.1), PDF e Book, https://www.gpo.gov/fdsys/pkg/CDOC-110hdoc50/pdf/CDOC-110hdoc50.pdf

14 *The Constitution of the United States of America*, Presented by Mr. Brady of Pennsylvania, July 25, 2007, (Washington, DC: Superintendent of Documents, Government Printing Office, 2007), 15 (Amendment XII), PDF e Book, https://www.gpo.gov/fdsys/pkg/CDOC-110hdoc50/pdf/CDOC-110hdoc50.pdf

15 Kevin Handy, Lisa Reigel, John Hagerson, and the Project Gutenberg Online Distributed Proofreading Team, *The Constitution of the United States of America: Analysis and Interpretation*, ed. Edward Corwin, Release Date: June 20, 2006, [eBook #18637], http://www.gutenberg.org/cache/epub/18637/pg18637.txt

16 Wikipedia contributors, "Money bill," *Wikipedia, The Free Encyclopedia,* https://en.wikipedia.org/w/index.php?title=Money_bill&oldid=879366831 (accessed April 5, 2019).

17 Wikipedia contributors, "House of Lords," *Wikipedia, The Free Encyclopedia,* https://en.wikipedia.org/w/index.php?title=House_of_Lords&oldid=890464735(accessed April 4, 2019).

18 *The Constitution of the United States of America*, Presented by Mr. Brady of Pennsylvania, July 25, 2007, (Washington, DC: Superintendent of Documents, Government Printing Office, 2007), 7 (Article II, Section 1.5), PDF e Book, https://www.gpo.gov/fdsys/pkg/CDOC-110hdoc50/pdf/CDOC-110hdoc50.pdf

19 *The Constitution of the United States of America*, Presented by Mr. Brady of Pennsylvania, July 25, 2007, (Washington, DC:

Superintendent of Documents, Government Printing Office, 2007), 2
(Article I, Section 2.2), PDF e Book,
https://www.gpo.gov/fdsys/pkg/CDOC-110hdoc50/pdf/CDOC-
110hdoc50.pdf

[20] *The Constitution of the United States of America*, Presented by Mr.
Brady of Pennsylvania, July 25, 2007, (Washington, DC:
Superintendent of Documents, Government Printing Office, 2007), 3
(Article I, Section 3.3), PDF e Book,
https://www.gpo.gov/fdsys/pkg/CDOC-110hdoc50/pdf/CDOC-
110hdoc50.pdf

[21] *The Constitution of the United States of America*, Presented by Mr.
Brady of Pennsylvania, July 25, 2007, (Washington, DC:
Superintendent of Documents, Government Printing Office, 2007), 8
(Article III, Section 1), PDF e Book,
https://www.gpo.gov/fdsys/pkg/CDOC-110hdoc50/pdf/CDOC-
110hdoc50.pdf

[22] It is not clear whether "natural" refers to someone born in the
republic or to someone born to a U.S. citizen anywhere in the world or
to someone born through a natural child birth.

[23] Wikipedia contributors, "List of Justices of the Supreme Court of
the United States," *Wikipedia, The Free
Encyclopedia,* https://en.wikipedia.org/w/index.php?title=List_of_Justi
ces_of_the_Supreme_Court_of_the_United_States&oldid=868421221
(accessed November 20, 2018).

[24] Wikipedia contributors, "Judicial Procedures Reform Bill of
1937," *Wikipedia, The Free
Encyclopedia,* https://en.wikipedia.org/w/index.php?title=Judicial_Pro
cedures_Reform_Bill_of_1937&oldid=842064985 (accessed May 21,
2018).

[25] "About the Supreme Court," *United States Courts*, August 26, 2016, http://www.uscourts.gov/about-federal-courts/educational-resources/about-educational-outreach/activity-resources/about

[26] Centers for Medicare and Medicaid Services, National Health Expenditure (NHE) Fact Sheet, accessed February 6, 2019, https://www.cms.gov/research-statistics-data-and-systems/statistics-trends-and-reports/nationalhealthexpenddata/nhe-fact-sheet.html

[27] Wikipedia contributors, "Mild cognitive impairment," *Wikipedia, The Free Encyclopedia,* https://en.wikipedia.org/w/index.php?title=Mild_cognitive_impairment&oldid=819373297 (accessed January 26, 2018).

[28] In 1986, the U.S. Congress abolished the mandatory retirement age by amending the Age Discrimination in Employment Act.

[29] Wikipedia contributors, "Citizens United v. FEC," *Wikipedia, The Free Encyclopedia,* accessed February 1, 2019, https://en.wikipedia.org/w/index.php?title=Citizens_United_v._FEC&oldid=823008900

[30] Wikisource contributors, "Constitution of the Fifth French Republic," *Wikisource ,* Title I, Article 2, accessed January 23, 2017, https://en.wikisource.org/w/index.php?title=Constitution_of_the_Fifth_French_Republic&oldid=6612441

[31] Wikisource contributors, "Basic Law for the Federal Republic of Germany," *Wikisource ,* Article 12a.(1), accessed January 21, 2017, https://en.wikisource.org/w/index.php?title=Basic_Law_for_the_Federal_Republic_of_Germany&oldid=5961088
Wikisource contributors, "Constitution of Russia," *Wikisource ,* Chapter 2, Article 59.2, accessed January 22, 2017, https://en.wikisource.org/w/index.php?title=Constitution_of_Russia&oldid=5445528.

[32] *The Constitution of the United States of America*, Presented by Mr. Brady of Pennsylvania, July 25, 2007, (Washington, DC: Superintendent of Documents, Government Printing Office, 2007), 3 (Article I, Section 5.2), PDF e Book, https://www.gpo.gov/fdsys/pkg/CDOC-110hdoc50/pdf/CDOC-110hdoc50.pdf

[33] Wikipedia contributors, "Cloture," *Wikipedia, The Free Encyclopedia,* https://en.wikipedia.org/w/index.php?title=Cloture&oldid=851139366 (accessed July 27, 2018).

[34] Wikipedia contributors, "Filibuster," *Wikipedia, The Free Encyclopedia,* https://en.wikipedia.org/w/index.php?title=Filibuster&oldid=851421625 (accessed July 27, 2018).

[35] Wikipedia contributors, "Filibuster in the United States Senate," *Wikipedia, The Free Encyclopedia,* https://en.wikipedia.org/w/index.php?title=Filibuster_in_the_United_States_Senate&oldid=849566473 (accessed July 27, 2018).

[36] Congressional Record Volume 146, Number 142 (Wednesday, November 1, 2000), Senate, page S11495, https://www.gpo.gov/fdsys/pkg/CREC-2000-11-01/html/CREC-2000-11-01-pt1-PgS11494-4.htm

[37] "U.S. Electoral College," *National Archives and Records Administration*, November 27, 2016, https://www.archives.gov/federal-register/electoral-college/about.html

[38] *The Constitution of the United States of America*, Presented by Mr. Brady of Pennsylvania, July 25, 2007, (Washington, DC: Superintendent of Documents, Government Printing Office, 2007), 6 (Article II, Section 1), 15 (Amendment XII), 23 (Amendment XXIII, Section 1), PDF e Book, https://www.gpo.gov/fdsys/pkg/CDOC-110hdoc50/pdf/CDOC-110hdoc50.pdf

[39] *The Constitution of the United States of America*, Presented by Mr. Brady of Pennsylvania, July 25, 2007, (Washington, DC: Superintendent of Documents, Government Printing Office, 2007), 9 (Article V), PDF e Book, https://www.gpo.gov/fdsys/pkg/CDOC-110hdoc50/pdf/CDOC-110hdoc50.pdf

[40] *The Constitution of the United States of America*, Presented by Mr. Brady of Pennsylvania, July 25, 2007, (Washington, DC: Superintendent of Documents, Government Printing Office, 2007), 9 (Article IV, Section 4), PDF e Book, https://www.gpo.gov/fdsys/pkg/CDOC-110hdoc50/pdf/CDOC-110hdoc50.pdf

[41] *The Constitution of the United States of America*, Presented by Mr. Brady of Pennsylvania, July 25, 2007, (Washington, DC: Superintendent of Documents, Government Printing Office, 2007), 14 (Amendment VII), PDF e Book, https://www.gpo.gov/fdsys/pkg/CDOC-110hdoc50/pdf/CDOC-110hdoc50.pdf

[42] *The Constitution of the United States of America*, Presented by Mr. Brady of Pennsylvania, July 25, 2007, (Washington, DC: Superintendent of Documents, Government Printing Office, 2007), 7 (Article II, Section 2.1), PDF e Book, https://www.gpo.gov/fdsys/pkg/CDOC-110hdoc50/pdf/CDOC-110hdoc50.pdf

[43] *The Constitution of the United States of America*, Presented by Mr. Brady of Pennsylvania, July 25, 2007, (Washington, DC: Superintendent of Documents, Government Printing Office, 2007), 8 (Article III, Section 2.3), PDF e Book, https://www.gpo.gov/fdsys/pkg/CDOC-110hdoc50/pdf/CDOC-110hdoc50.pdf

[44] Mark Twain, *Roughing It* 1880, Release Date: August 18, 2006 [EBook #3177], Last Updated: February 24, 2018, Chapter XLVIII, http://www.gutenberg.org/files/3177/3177-0.txt

⁴⁵ Wikipedia contributors, "Parliament of Great Britain," *Wikipedia, The Free Encyclopedia,* https://en.wikipedia.org/w/index.php?title=Parliament_of_Great_Britain&oldid=878746571 (accessed April 7, 2019).

⁴⁶ Wikipedia contributors, "Majority government," *Wikipedia, The Free Encyclopedia,* https://en.wikipedia.org/w/index.php?title=Majority_government&oldid=811875210 (accessed February 14, 2018).

⁴⁷ "Hung Parliament," *U.K. Parliament Homepage*, November 24, 2018, https://www.parliament.uk/about/how/elections-and-voting/general/hung-parliament/

⁴⁸ Wikipedia contributors, "Coalition government," *Wikipedia, The Free Encyclopedia,* https://en.wikipedia.org/w/index.php?title=Coalition_government&oldid=822698641 (accessed February 14, 2018).

⁴⁹ Wikipedia contributors, "Confidence and supply," *Wikipedia, The Free Encyclopedia,* https://en.wikipedia.org/w/index.php?title=Confidence_and_supply&oldid=888715229 (accessed April 6, 2019).

⁵⁰ Wikipedia contributors, "Hung parliament," *Wikipedia, The Free Encyclopedia,* https://en.wikipedia.org/w/index.php?title=Hung_parliament&oldid=816106187 (accessed February 14, 2018).

⁵¹ "Parliamentary sovereignty," *U.K. Parliament Home Page*, September 1, 2016, http://www.parliament.uk/about/how/sovereignty/

⁵² "Judicial Review", *Courts and Tribunals Judiciary*, November 25, 2018, https://www.judiciary.uk/you-and-the-judiciary/judicial-review/

⁵³ Aristotle, *Politics A Treatise on Government*, trans. William Ellis, (Produced by Eric Eldred, and David Widger, Release Date: June 5,

2009 [E Book # 6962], Last updated: January 12, 2013), Book II, Chapter I, http://www.gutenberg.org/files/6762/6762-h/6762-h.htm#link2HCH0019

[54] "America's Founding Documents," *National Archives*. (Last reviewed: September 25, 2018). https://www.archives.gov/founding-docs/constitution-q-and-a

[55] Wikipedia contributors, "List of Presidents of the United States by education," *Wikipedia, The Free Encyclopedia,* https://en.wikipedia.org/w/index.php?title=List_of_Pres idents_of_the_United_States_by_education&oldid=826767506 (access ed March 13, 2018).

[56] Wikipedia contributors, "James Madison," *Wikipedia, The Free Encyclopedia,* https://en.wikipedia.org/w/index.php?title=James_Madison&oldid=88 5906395 (accessed March 5, 2019).

[57] *The Constitution of the United States of America*, Presented by Mr. Brady of Pennsylvania, July 25, 2007, (Washington, DC: Superintendent of Documents, Government Printing Office, 2007), 1 (Preamble), PDF e Book, https://www.gpo.gov/fdsys/pkg/CDOC-110hdoc50/pdf/CDOC-110hdoc50.pdf

[58] Wikisource contributors, "Constitution of the Fifth French Republic," *Wikisource ,* Title I, Article 2, accessed January 23, 2017, https://en.wikisource.org/w/index.php?title=Constitution_of_the_Fifth _French_Republic&oldid=6612441

[59] Ibid.

[60] Ibid.

[61] Wikisource contributors, "Constitution of Russia," *Wikisource ,* Chapter 1, Article 4.2, accessed January 22, 2017,

https://en.wikisource.org/w/index.php?title=Constitution_of_Russia&oldid=5445528

[62] Wikisource contributors, "Constitution of Russia," *Wikisource* , Chapter 1, Article 15.1, accessed January 22, 2017, https://en.wikisource.org/w/index.php?title=Constitution_of_Russia&oldid=5445528

[63] *The Constitution of the United States of America*, Presented by Mr. Brady of Pennsylvania, July 25, 2007, (Washington, DC: Superintendent of Documents, Government Printing Office, 2007), 10 (Article VI.2), PDF e Book, https://www.gpo.gov/fdsys/pkg/CDOC-110hdoc50/pdf/CDOC-110hdoc50.pdf

[64] Wikisource contributors, "Constitution of Russia," *Wikisource* , Chapter 1, Articles 13.2, 14.1, accessed January 22, 2017, https://en.wikisource.org/w/index.php?title=Constitution_of_Russia&oldid=5445528

[65] Wikisource contributors, "Constitution of Russia," *Wikisource* , Chapter 2, Article 19.1, accessed January 22, 2017, https://en.wikisource.org/w/index.php?title=Constitution_of_Russia&oldid=5445528

[66] Wikisource contributors, "Constitution of the Fifth French Republic," *Wikisource* , Title I, Article 4, accessed January 23, 2017, https://en.wikisource.org/w/index.php?title=Constitution_of_the_Fifth_French_Republic&oldid=6612441

[67] *The Constitution of the United States of America*, Presented by Mr. Brady of Pennsylvania, July 25, 2007, (Washington, DC: Superintendent of Documents, Government Printing Office, 2007), 13 (Amendment I), PDF e Book, https://www.gpo.gov/fdsys/pkg/CDOC-110hdoc50/pdf/CDOC-110hdoc50.pdf

[68] Wikisource contributors, "Constitution of Russia," *Wikisource* , Chapter 2, Article 27.1, accessed November 28, 2018,

https://en.wikisource.org/w/index.php?title=Constitution_of_Russia&oldid=5445528

[69] *The Constitution of the United States of America*, Presented by Mr. Brady of Pennsylvania, July 25, 2007, (Washington, DC: Superintendent of Documents, Government Printing Office, 2007), 26 (Amendment XXVI), PDF e Book, https://www.gpo.gov/fdsys/pkg/CDOC-110hdoc50/pdf/CDOC-110hdoc50.pdf

[70] Wikipedia contributors, "Community property," *Wikipedia, The Free Encyclopedia,* https://en.wikipedia.org/w/index.php?title=Community_property&oldid=881094543 (accessed February 17, 2019).

[71] *The Constitution of the United States of America*, Presented by Mr. Brady of Pennsylvania, July 25, 2007, (Washington, DC: Superintendent of Documents, Government Printing Office, 2007), 5 (Article I, Section 8.6), PDF e Book, https://www.gpo.gov/fdsys/pkg/CDOC-110hdoc50/pdf/CDOC-110hdoc50.pdf

[72] As of 30 November 2018, the population density of the world (excluding Antarctica) was 57 persons/square kilometer. This was rounded off to 60 persons/square kilometer. Wikipedia contributors, "List of countries and dependencies by population density," *Wikipedia, The Free Encyclopedia,* https://en.wikipedia.org/w/index.php?title=List_of_countries_and_dependencies_by_population_density&oldid=740737910 (accessed November 30, 2018).

[73] *The Constitution of the United States of America*, Presented by Mr. Brady of Pennsylvania, July 25, 2007, (Washington, DC: Superintendent of Documents, Government Printing Office, 2007), 13 (Amendment II), PDF e Book, https://www.gpo.gov/fdsys/pkg/CDOC-110hdoc50/pdf/CDOC-110hdoc50.pdf

[74] Wikipedia contributors, "Hatch Act of 1939," *Wikipedia, The Free Encyclopedia,* https://en.wikipedia.org/w/index.php?title=Hatch_Act_of_1939&oldid=874556119(accessed February 18, 2019).

[75] *The Constitution of the United States of America*, Presented by Mr. Brady of Pennsylvania, July 25, 2007, (Washington, DC: Superintendent of Documents, Government Printing Office, 2007), 16 (Amendment XIV, Section 1), PDF e Book, https://www.gpo.gov/fdsys/pkg/CDOC-110hdoc50/pdf/CDOC-110hdoc50.pdf

[76] Wikisource contributors, "Constitution of Russia," *Wikisource ,* Chapter 2, Article 35.4, accessed January 22, 2017, https://en.wikisource.org/w/index.php?title=Constitution_of_Russia&oldid=5445528

[77] Wikisource contributors, "Constitution of Russia," *Wikisource ,* Chapter 2, Article 57, accessed January 22 2017, https://en.wikisource.org/w/index.php?title=Constitution_of_Russia&oldid=5445528

[78] *The Constitution of the United States of America*, Presented by Mr. Brady of Pennsylvania, July 25, 2007, (Washington, DC: Superintendent of Documents, Government Printing Office, 2007), 5 (Article I, Section 9.5), PDF e Book, https://www.gpo.gov/fdsys/pkg/CDOC-110hdoc50/pdf/CDOC-110hdoc50.pdf

[79] "How can I stand in an election?," *U.K. Parliament Home Page*, September 6, 2016, http://www.parliament.uk/get-involved/elections/standing/

[80] Wikipedia contributors, "Logan Act," *Wikipedia, The Free Encyclopedia,* https://en.wikipedia.org/w/index.php?title=Logan_Act&oldid=813330099 (accessed December 3, 2017).

81 Wikisource contributors, "Constitution of Russia," *Wikisource ,* Chapter 1, Articles 6.2, 6.3, accessed January 22, 2017, https://en.wikisource.org/w/index.php?title=Constitution_of_Russia&oldid=5445528

82 *The Constitution of the United States of America*, Presented by Mr. Brady of Pennsylvania, July 25, 2007, (Washington, DC: Superintendent of Documents, Government Printing Office, 2007), 7 (Article II, Section 2.2), PDF e Book, https://www.gpo.gov/fdsys/pkg/CDOC-110hdoc50/pdf/CDOC-110hdoc50.pdf

83 *The Constitution of the United States of America*, Presented by Mr. Brady of Pennsylvania, July 25, 2007, (Washington, DC: Superintendent of Documents, Government Printing Office, 2007), 2 (Article I, Section 2.3), PDF e Book, https://www.gpo.gov/fdsys/pkg/CDOC-110hdoc50/pdf/CDOC-110hdoc50.pdf

84 *The Constitution of the United States of America*, Presented by Mr. Brady of Pennsylvania, July 25, 2007, (Washington, DC: Superintendent of Documents, Government Printing Office, 2007), 16 (Amendment XIII), PDF e Book, https://www.gpo.gov/fdsys/pkg/CDOC-110hdoc50/pdf/CDOC-110hdoc50.pdf

85 *The Constitution of the United States of America*, Presented by Mr. Brady of Pennsylvania, July 25, 2007, (Washington, DC: Superintendent of Documents, Government Printing Office, 2007), 5 (Article I, Section 9.2), PDF e Book, https://www.gpo.gov/fdsys/pkg/CDOC-110hdoc50/pdf/CDOC-110hdoc50.pdf

86 *The Constitution of the United States of America*, Presented by Mr. Brady of Pennsylvania, July 25, 2007, (Washington, DC: Superintendent of Documents, Government Printing Office, 2007), 6

(Article I, Section 9.7), PDF e Book,
https://www.gpo.gov/fdsys/pkg/CDOC-110hdoc50/pdf/CDOC-110hdoc50.pdf

[87] *The Constitution of the United States of America*, Presented by Mr. Brady of Pennsylvania, July 25, 2007, (Washington, DC: Superintendent of Documents, Government Printing Office, 2007), 7 (Article II, Section 2.2), PDF e Book, https://www.gpo.gov/fdsys/pkg/CDOC-110hdoc50/pdf/CDOC-110hdoc50.pdf

[88]*The Constitution of the United States of America*, Presented by Mr. Brady of Pennsylvania, July 25, 2007, (Washington, DC: Superintendent of Documents, Government Printing Office, 2007), 6 (Article I, Section 10.3), PDF e Book, https://www.gpo.gov/fdsys/pkg/CDOC-110hdoc50/pdf/CDOC-110hdoc50.pdf

[89] Wikisource contributors, "Constitution of the Fifth French Republic," *Wikisource* , Title IV, Article 26, accessed January 23, 2017, https://en.wikisource.org/w/index.php?title=Constitution_of_the_Fifth_French_Republic&oldid=6612441

[90] Wikipedia contributors, "TRIPS Agreement," *Wikipedia, The Free Encyclopedia,* https://en.wikipedia.org/w/index.php?title=TRIPS_Agreement&oldid=726438281 (accessed June 22, 2016).

[91] *The Constitution of the United States of America*, Presented by Mr. Brady of Pennsylvania, July 25, 2007, (Washington, DC: Superintendent of Documents, Government Printing Office, 2007), 14 (Amendment V), PDF e Book, https://www.gpo.gov/fdsys/pkg/CDOC-110hdoc50/pdf/CDOC-110hdoc50.pdf

92 Wikisource contributors, "Basic Law for the Federal Republic of Germany," *Wikisource*, Article 87C, accessed January 14, 2017, https://en.wikisource.org/w/index.php?title=Basic_Law_for_the_Federal_Republic_of_Germany&oldid=5961088

93 Wikisource contributors, "Basic Law for the Federal Republic of Germany," *Wikisource*, Articles 87d and 87e, accessed January 19, 2017, https://en.wikisource.org/w/index.php?title=Basic_Law_for_the_Federal_Republic_of_Germany&oldid=5961088

94 Wikisource contributors, "Basic Law for the Federal Republic of Germany," *Wikisource*, Article 87f, accessed January 19, 2017, https://en.wikisource.org/w/index.php?title=Basic_Law_for_the_Federal_Republic_of_Germany&oldid=5961088

95 Wikisource contributors, "Basic Law for the Federal Republic of Germany," *Wikisource*, Article 89, accessed January 19, 2017, https://en.wikisource.org/w/index.php?title=Basic_Law_for_the_Federal_Republic_of_Germany&oldid=5961088

96 Wikisource contributors, "Basic Law for the Federal Republic of Germany," *Wikisource*, Article 90, accessed January 19, 2017, https://en.wikisource.org/w/index.php?title=Basic_Law_for_the_Federal_Republic_of_Germany&oldid=5961088

97 Wikisource contributors, "Basic Law for the Federal Republic of Germany," *Wikisource*, Article 91c, accessed January 19, 2017, https://en.wikisource.org/w/index.php?title=Basic_Law_for_the_Federal_Republic_of_Germany&oldid=5961088

98 *The Constitution of the United States of America*, Presented by Mr. Brady of Pennsylvania, July 25, 2007, (Washington, DC: Superintendent of Documents, Government Printing Office, 2007), 8 (Article II, Section 3), PDF e Book, https://www.gpo.gov/fdsys/pkg/CDOC-110hdoc50/pdf/CDOC-110hdoc50.pdf

[99]*The Constitution of the United States of America*, Presented by Mr. Brady of Pennsylvania, July 25, 2007, (Washington, DC: Superintendent of Documents, Government Printing Office, 2007), 6 (Article II, Section 1.1), PDF e Book, https://www.gpo.gov/fdsys/pkg/CDOC-110hdoc50/pdf/CDOC-110hdoc50.pdf

[100] *The Constitution of the United States of America*, Presented by Mr. Brady of Pennsylvania, July 25, 2007, (Washington, DC: Superintendent of Documents, Government Printing Office, 2007), 7 (Article II, Section 2.1), PDF e Book, https://www.gpo.gov/fdsys/pkg/CDOC-110hdoc50/pdf/CDOC-110hdoc50.pdf

[101] Wikisource contributors, "Constitution of Russia," *Wikisource ,* Chapter 4, Article 80.2, accessed January 22, 2017, https://en.wikisource.org/w/index.php?title=Constitution_of_Russia&oldid=5445528

[102]*The Constitution of the United States of America*, Presented by Mr. Brady of Pennsylvania, July 25, 2007, (Washington, DC: Superintendent of Documents, Government Printing Office, 2007), 7 (Article II, Section 1.8), PDF e Book, https://www.gpo.gov/fdsys/pkg/CDOC-110hdoc50/pdf/CDOC-110hdoc50.pdf

[103]*The Constitution of the United States of America*, Presented by Mr. Brady of Pennsylvania, July 25, 2007, (Washington, DC: Superintendent of Documents, Government Printing Office, 2007), 24 (Amendment XXV, Section 1), PDF e Book, https://www.gpo.gov/fdsys/pkg/CDOC-110hdoc50/pdf/CDOC-110hdoc50.pdf

[104] Wikisource contributors, "Constitution of Russia," *Wikisource ,* Chapter 4, Article 80.3, accessed January 22, 2017,

https://en.wikisource.org/w/index.php?title=Constitution_of_Russia&o
ldid=5445528

[105] *The Constitution of the United States of America*, Presented by Mr. Brady of Pennsylvania, July 25, 2007, (Washington, DC: Superintendent of Documents, Government Printing Office, 2007), 26 (Amendment XXVII), PDF e Book, https://www.gpo.gov/fdsys/pkg/CDOC-110hdoc50/pdf/CDOC-110hdoc50.pdf

[106] Wikisource contributors, "Constitution of the Fifth French Republic," *Wikisource* , Title V, Article 37, accessed January 23, 2017, https://en.wikisource.org/w/index.php?title=Constitution_of_the_Fifth_French_Republic&oldid=6612441

[107]Wikipedia contributors, "Money bill," *Wikipedia, The Free Encyclopedia,* https://en.wikipedia.org/w/index.php?title=Money_bill&oldid=879366831 (accessed April 4, 2019).

[108] *The Constitution of the United States of America*, Presented by Mr. Brady of Pennsylvania, July 25, 2007, (Washington, DC: Superintendent of Documents, Government Printing Office, 2007), 5 (Article I, Section 9.3), PDF e Book, https://www.gpo.gov/fdsys/pkg/CDOC-110hdoc50/pdf/CDOC-110hdoc50.pdf

[109] Wikisource contributors, "Constitution of Russia," *Wikisource* , Chapter 2, Article 34.2, accessed January 22, 2017, https://en.wikisource.org/w/index.php?title=Constitution_of_Russia&o
ldid=5445528

[110] *The Constitution of the United States of America*, Presented by Mr. Brady of Pennsylvania, July 25, 2007, (Washington, DC: Superintendent of Documents, Government Printing Office, 2007), 4 (Article I, Section 8.3), PDF e Book,

https://www.gpo.gov/fdsys/pkg/CDOC-110hdoc50/pdf/CDOC-110hdoc50.pdf

[111] Wikisource contributors, "Constitution of Russia," *Wikisource ,* Chapter 1, Article 7.2, accessed January 22, 2017, https://en.wikisource.org/w/index.php?title=Constitution_of_Russia&oldid=5445528

[112] "Office and Role of Speaker," *U.K. Parliament Home Page,* September 12, 2016, http://www.parliament.uk/business/commons/the-Speaker/the-role-of-the-Speaker/role-of-the-Speaker/

[113] Wikisource contributors, "Constitution of the Fifth French Republic," *Wikisource ,* Title IV, Article 27, accessed January 23, 2017, https://en.wikisource.org/w/index.php?title=Constitution_of_the_Fifth_French_Republic&oldid=6612441

[114] Wikisource contributors, "Constitution of the Fifth French Republic," *Wikisource ,* Title IV, Article 33, accessed January 23, 2017, https://en.wikisource.org/w/index.php?title=Constitution_of_the_Fifth_French_Republic&oldid=6612441

[115] *The Constitution of the United States of America*, Presented by Mr. Brady of Pennsylvania, July 25, 2007, (Washington, DC: Superintendent of Documents, Government Printing Office, 2007), 3 (Article I, Section 5.1), PDF e Book, https://www.gpo.gov/fdsys/pkg/CDOC-110hdoc50/pdf/CDOC-110hdoc50.pdf

[116] *The Constitution of the United States of America*, Presented by Mr. Brady of Pennsylvania, July 25, 2007, (Washington, DC: Superintendent of Documents, Government Printing Office, 2007), 3 (Article I, Section 5.2), PDF e Book,

https://www.gpo.gov/fdsys/pkg/CDOC-110hdoc50/pdf/CDOC-110hdoc50.pdf

[117] *The Constitution of the United States of America*, Presented by Mr. Brady of Pennsylvania, July 25, 2007, (Washington, DC: Superintendent of Documents, Government Printing Office, 2007), 4 (Article I, Section 8.1), PDF e Book, https://www.gpo.gov/fdsys/pkg/CDOC-110hdoc50/pdf/CDOC-110hdoc50.pdf

[118] *The Constitution of the United States of America*, Presented by Mr. Brady of Pennsylvania, July 25, 2007, (Washington, DC: Superintendent of Documents, Government Printing Office, 2007), 5 (Article I, Section 9.3), PDF e Book, https://www.gpo.gov/fdsys/pkg/CDOC-110hdoc50/pdf/CDOC-110hdoc50.pdf

[119] *The Constitution of the United States of America*, Presented by Mr. Brady of Pennsylvania, July 25, 2007, (Washington, DC: Superintendent of Documents, Government Printing Office, 2007), 4 (Article I, Section 7.2), PDF e Book, https://www.gpo.gov/fdsys/pkg/CDOC-110hdoc50/pdf/CDOC-110hdoc50.pdf

[120] "Passage of a Bill," *U.K. Parliament Home Page*, September 15, 2016, http://www.parliament.uk/about/how/laws/passage-bill/

[121] *The Constitution of the United States of America*, Presented by Mr. Brady of Pennsylvania, July 25, 2007, (Washington, DC: Superintendent of Documents, Government Printing Office, 2007), 3 (Article I, Section 5.2), PDF e Book, https://www.gpo.gov/fdsys/pkg/CDOC-110hdoc50/pdf/CDOC-110hdoc50.pdf

[122] *The Constitution of the United States of America*, Presented by Mr. Brady of Pennsylvania, July 25, 2007, (Washington, DC: Superintendent of Documents, Government Printing Office, 2007), 5

(Article I, Section 8.11), PDF e Book,
https://www.gpo.gov/fdsys/pkg/CDOC-110hdoc50/pdf/CDOC-110hdoc50.pdf

[123] *The Constitution of the United States of America*, Presented by Mr. Brady of Pennsylvania, July 25, 2007, (Washington, DC: Superintendent of Documents, Government Printing Office, 2007), 7 (Article II, Section 2.2), PDF e Book,
https://www.gpo.gov/fdsys/pkg/CDOC-110hdoc50/pdf/CDOC-110hdoc50.pdf

[124] Wikipedia contributors, "Civil law (legal system)," *Wikipedia, The Free Encyclopedia,* https://en.wikipedia.org/w/index.php?title=Civil_law_(legal_system)&oldid=882739889 (accessed February 14, 2019).

[125] *The Constitution of the United States of America*, Presented by Mr. Brady of Pennsylvania, July 25, 2007, (Washington, DC: Superintendent of Documents, Government Printing Office, 2007), 8 (Article III, Section 2.1), PDF e Book,
https://www.gpo.gov/fdsys/pkg/CDOC-110hdoc50/pdf/CDOC-110hdoc50.pdf

[126] Wikipedia contributors, "Judiciary of Germany," *Wikipedia, The Free Encyclopedia,* https://en.wikipedia.org/w/index.php?title=Judiciary_of_Germany&oldid=879389996 (accessed February 16, 2019).

[127] Wikipedia contributors, "Prosecutor," *Wikipedia, The Free Encyclopedia,* https://en.wikipedia.org/w/index.php?title=Prosecutor&oldid=875512489 (accessed December 30, 2018).

[128] The French Legal System, (Edited by Ministry of Justice /2012), 10 (The administration of proof under French criminal law), http://www.justice.gouv.fr/art_pix/french_legal_system.pdf (accessed February 25, 2019).

[129] Wikipedia contributors, "Brady v. Maryland," *Wikipedia, The Free Encyclopedia,* https://en.wikipedia.org/w/index.php?title=Brady_v._Maryland&oldid=877256570(accessed March 15, 2019).

[130] Wikipedia contributors, "Appellate jurisdiction," *Wikipedia, The Free Encyclopedia,* https://en.wikipedia.org/w/index.php?title=Appellate_jurisdiction&oldid=882980081 (accessed February 23, 2019).

[131] *The Constitution of the United States of America*, Presented by Mr. Brady of Pennsylvania, July 25, 2007, (Washington, DC: Superintendent of Documents, Government Printing Office, 2007), 8 (Article II, Section 2.2), PDF e Book, https://www.gpo.gov/fdsys/pkg/CDOC-110hdoc50/pdf/CDOC-110hdoc50.pdf

[132] *The Constitution of the United States of America*, Presented by Mr. Brady of Pennsylvania, July 25, 2007, (Washington, DC: Superintendent of Documents, Government Printing Office, 2007), 8 (Article III, Section 2.3), PDF e Book, https://www.gpo.gov/fdsys/pkg/CDOC-110hdoc50/pdf/CDOC-110hdoc50.pdf

[133] *The Constitution of the United States of America*, Presented by Mr. Brady of Pennsylvania, July 25, 2007, (Washington, DC: Superintendent of Documents, Government Printing Office, 2007), 9 (Article IV, Section 2.2), PDF e Book, https://www.gpo.gov/fdsys/pkg/CDOC-110hdoc50/pdf/CDOC-110hdoc50.pdf

[134] *The Constitution of the United States of America*, Presented by Mr. Brady of Pennsylvania, July 25, 2007, (Washington, DC: Superintendent of Documents, Government Printing Office, 2007), 14 (Amendment VI), PDF e Book, https://www.gpo.gov/fdsys/pkg/CDOC-110hdoc50/pdf/CDOC-110hdoc50.pdf

[135] *The Constitution of the United States of America*, Presented by Mr. Brady of Pennsylvania, July 25, 2007, (Washington, DC: Superintendent of Documents, Government Printing Office, 2007), 8 (Article III, Section 2.3), PDF e Book, https://www.gpo.gov/fdsys/pkg/CDOC-110hdoc50/pdf/CDOC-110hdoc50.pdf

[136] Wikisource contributors, "Constitution of Russia," *Wikisource, Chapter 2, Article 49.1,* accessed December 13, 2018, https://en.wikisource.org/w/index.php?title=Constitution_of_Russia&oldid=5445528

[137] *The Constitution of the United States of America*, Presented by Mr. Brady of Pennsylvania, July 25, 2007, (Washington, DC: Superintendent of Documents, Government Printing Office, 2007), 13 (Amendment IV), PDF e Book, https://www.gpo.gov/fdsys/pkg/CDOC-110hdoc50/pdf/CDOC-110hdoc50.pdf

[138] *The Constitution of the United States of America*, Presented by Mr. Brady of Pennsylvania, July 25, 2007, (Washington, DC: Superintendent of Documents, Government Printing Office, 2007), 14 (Amendment VI), PDF e Book, https://www.gpo.gov/fdsys/pkg/CDOC-110hdoc50/pdf/CDOC-110hdoc50.pdf

[139] Wikisource contributors, "Constitution of Russia," *Wikisource ,* Chapter 2, Article   22.2, accessed January 22, 2017, https://en.wikisource.org/w/index.php?title=Constitution_of_Russia&oldid=5445528

[140] Japan, *The Constitution of Japan, 1946,* Posting date: July 26, 2008, Chapter III, Article 38, (Japan: 1946), E Book # 612, http://www.gutenberg.org/cache/epub/612/pg612.txt

[141] Japan, *The Constitution of Japan, 1946,* Posting date: July 26, 2008, Chapter III, Article 39, (Japan: 1946), E Book # 612, http://www.gutenberg.org/cache/epub/612/pg612.txt

[142] Japan, *The Constitution of Japan, 1946,* Posting date: July 26, 2008, Chapter III, Article 40, (Japan: 1946), E Book # 612, http://www.gutenberg.org/cache/epub/612/pg612.txt

[143] *The Constitution of the United States of America*, Presented by Mr. Brady of Pennsylvania, July 25, 2007, (Washington, DC: Superintendent of Documents, Government Printing Office, 2007), 14 (Amendment V), PDF e Book, https://www.gpo.gov/fdsys/pkg/CDOC-110hdoc50/pdf/CDOC-110hdoc50.pdf

[144] Office of the United States Attorneys, Initial Hearing/ Arraignment, https://www.justice.gov/usao/justice-101/initial-hearing (accessed February 9, 2019).

[145] Office of the United States Attorneys, Preliminary Hearing, https://www.justice.gov/usao/justice-101/preliminary-hearing (accessed February 9, 2019).

[146] Wikipedia contributors, "Preliminary hearing," *Wikipedia, The Free Encyclopedia,* https://en.wikipedia.org/w/index.php?title=Preliminary_hearing&oldid=878582210 (accessed February 10, 2019).

[147] Wikipedia contributors, "Speedy Trial Act," *Wikipedia, The Free Encyclopedia,* https://en.wikipedia.org/w/index.php?title=Speedy_Trial_Act&oldid=831132653(accessed December 22, 2018).

[148] *The Constitution of the United States of America*, Presented by Mr. Brady of Pennsylvania, July 25, 2007, (Washington, DC: Superintendent of Documents, Government Printing Office, 2007), 14 (Amendment VIII), PDF e Book,

https://www.gpo.gov/fdsys/pkg/CDOC-110hdoc50/pdf/CDOC-110hdoc50.pdf

[149] Ibid.

[150] Wikisource contributors, "Constitution of Russia," *Wikisource*, Chapter 2, Article   53, accessed January 22, 2017, https://en.wikisource.org/w/index.php?title=Constitution_of_Russia&oldid=5445528

[151] *The Constitution of the United States of America*, Presented by Mr. Brady of Pennsylvania, July 25, 2007, (Washington, DC: Superintendent of Documents, Government Printing Office, 2007), 13 (Amendment III), PDF e Book, https://www.gpo.gov/fdsys/pkg/CDOC-110hdoc50/pdf/CDOC-110hdoc50.pdf

[152] Wikisource contributors, "Constitution of Russia," *Wikisource*, Chapter 2, Article   43.4, accessed January 22, 2017, https://en.wikisource.org/w/index.php?title=Constitution_of_Russia&oldid=5445528

[153] Wikisource contributors, "Constitution of Russia," *Wikisource*, Chapter 2, Article   43.5, accessed January 22, 2017, https://en.wikisource.org/w/index.php?title=Constitution_of_Russia&oldid=5445528

[154] Wikipedia contributors, "Homeschooling international status and statistics," *Wikipedia, The Free Encyclopedia,* https://en.wikipedia.org/w/index.php?title=Homeschooling_international_status_and_statistics&oldid=755304804 (accessed December 17, 2016).

[155] Micra, Inc., Plainfield, N.J., *1913 Webster's Unabridged Dictionary version 0.50 Letters A and B,* (Springfield, Mass.: C. & G. Merriam

Co., 1913), Last Edited: February 11, 1999 [E Text #660], http://www.gutenberg.org/cache/epub/660/pg660.txt

[156] Ibid.

[157] Ibid.

[158] Ibid.

[159] Ibid.

[160] Ibid.

[161] Wikipedia contributors, "Appeal," *Wikipedia, The Free Encyclopedia,* https://en.wikipedia.org/w/index.php?title=Appeal&oldid=808544305 (accessed April 12, 2018).

[162] Wikipedia contributors, "Appellate court," *Wikipedia, The Free Encyclopedia,* https://en.wikipedia.org/w/index.php?title=Appellate_court&oldid=869031337(accessed December 21, 2018).

[163] Wikipedia contributors, "Appellate jurisdiction," *Wikipedia, The Free Encyclopedia,* https://en.wikipedia.org/w/index.php?title=Appellate_jurisdiction&oldid=873900099 (accessed December 21, 2018).

[164] Micra, Inc., Plainfield, N.J., *1913 Webster's Unabridged Dictionary version 0.50 Letters A and B,* (Springfield, Mass.: C. & G. Merriam Co., 1913), Last Edited: February 11, 1999 [E Text #660], http://www.gutenberg.org/cache/epub/660/pg660.txt

[165] Ibid.

[166] Wikipedia contributors, "Arbitration," *Wikipedia, The Free Encyclopedia,* https://en.wikipedia.org/w/index.php?title=Arbitration&oldid=874607588 (accessed December 21, 2018).

[167] Micra, Inc., Plainfield, N.J., *1913 Webster's Unabridged Dictionary version 0.50 Letters A and B,* (Springfield, Mass.: C. & G. Merriam

Co., 1913), Last Edited: February 11, 1999 [E Text #660],
http://www.gutenberg.org/cache/epub/660/pg660.txt

168 Wikipedia contributors, "Arraignment," *Wikipedia, The Free Encyclopedia,* https://en.wikipedia.org/w/index.php?title=Arraignment&oldid=868461715 (accessed December 22, 2018).

169 Micra, Inc., Plainfield, N.J., *1913 Webster's Unabridged Dictionary version 0.50 Letters A and B,* (Springfield, Mass.: C. & G. Merriam Co., 1913), Last Edited: February 11, 1999 [E Text #660],
http://www.gutenberg.org/cache/epub/660/pg660.txt

170 Wikipedia contributors, "BC," *Wikipedia, The Free Encyclopedia,* https://en.wikipedia.org/w/index.php?title=BC&oldid=891540634 (accessed April 25, 2019).

171 Micra, Inc., Plainfield, N.J., *1913 Webster's Unabridged Dictionary version 0.50 Letters A and B,* (Springfield, Mass.: C. & G. Merriam Co., 1913), Last Edited: February 11, 1999 [E Text #660],
http://www.gutenberg.org/cache/epub/660/pg660.txt

172 Ibid.

173 Wikipedia contributors, "Bill (law)," *Wikipedia, The Free Encyclopedia,*
https://en.wikipedia.org/w/index.php?title=Bill_(law)&oldid=809065686 (accessed November 8, 2017).

174 Micra, Inc., Plainfield, N.J., *1913 Webster's Unabridged Dictionary version 0.50 Letter C* (Springfield, Mass.: C. & G. Merriam Co., 1913), Last Edited: February 11, 1999 [E Text #661],
http://www.gutenberg.org/cache/epub/661/pg661.txt

175 Wikipedia contributors, "Chain migration," *Wikipedia, The Free Encyclopedia,*

https://en.wikipedia.org/w/index.php?title=Chain_migration&oldid=79 9117482 (accessed December 27, 2018).

176 Wikipedia contributors, "Separation of powers," *Wikipedia, The Free Encyclopedia,* https://en.wikipedia.org/w/index.php?title=Separation_ of_powers&oldid=852415515 (accessed August 6, 2018).

177 Micra, Inc., Plainfield, N.J., *1913 Webster's Unabridged Dictionary version 0.50 Letter C* (Springfield, Mass.: C. & G. Merriam Co., 1913), Last Edited: February 11, 1999 [E Text #661], http://www.gutenberg.org/cache/epub/661/pg661.txt

178 Wikipedia contributors, "Civil law (common law)," *Wikipedia, The Free Encyclopedia,* https://en.wikipedia.org/w/index.php?title=Civil_law_(c ommon_law)&oldid=861010710 (accessed January 8, 2019).

179 Wikipedia contributors, "Cloture," *Wikipedia, The Free Encyclopedia,* https://en.wikipedia.org/w/index.php?title=Cloture&oldid=829250830 (accessed April 19, 2018).

180 Micra, Inc., Plainfield, N.J., *1913 Webster's Unabridged Dictionary version 0.50 Letter C* (Springfield, Mass.: C. & G. Merriam Co., 1913), Last Edited: February 11, 1999 [E Text #661], http://www.gutenberg.org/cache/epub/661/pg661.txt

181 Ibid.

182 Ibid.

183 Ibid.

184 Ibid.

185 Ibid.

[186] Wikipedia contributors, "Court order," *Wikipedia, The Free Encyclopedia,* https://en.wikipedia.org/w/index.php?title=Court_order&oldid=823212026 (accessed January 11, 2019).

[187] Wikipedia contributors, "Crime," *Wikipedia, The Free Encyclopedia,* https://en.wikipedia.org/w/index.php?title=Crime&oldid=826807704 (accessed March 30, 2018).

[188] Micra, Inc., Plainfield, N.J., *1913 Webster's Unabridged Dictionary version 0.50 Letter C* (Springfield, Mass.: C. & G. Merriam Co., 1913), Last Edited: February 11, 1999 [E Text #661], http://www.gutenberg.org/cache/epub/661/pg661.txt

[189] Micra, Inc., Plainfield, N.J., *1913 Webster's Unabridged Dictionary version 0.50 Letters D and E* (Springfield, Mass.: C. & G. Merriam Co., 1913), Last Edited: February 11, 1999 [E Text #662], http://www.gutenberg.org/cache/epub/662/pg662.txt

[190] Wikipedia contributors, "United States district court," *Wikipedia, The Free Encyclopedia,* https://en.wikipedia.org/w/index.php?title=United_States_district_court&oldid=854100832 (accessed August 23, 2018).

[191] Wikipedia contributors, "Due process," *Wikipedia, The Free Encyclopedia,* https://en.wikipedia.org/w/index.php?title=Due_process&oldid=850463384 (accessed September 3, 2018).

[192] Wikipedia contributors, "Duty (economics)," *Wikipedia, The Free Encyclopedia,* https://en.wikipedia.org/w/index.php?title=Duty_(economics)&oldid=825053252(accessed April 12, 2018).

[193] Wikipedia contributors, "Eminent domain," *Wikipedia, The Free Encyclopedia,* https://en.wikipedia.org/w/index.php?title=Eminent_domain&oldid=780849342 (accessed June 3, 2017)

194 Micra, Inc., Plainfield, N.J., *1913 Webster's Unabridged Dictionary version 0.50 Letters D and E* (Springfield, Mass.: C. & G. Merriam Co., 1913), Last Edited: February 11, 1999 [E Text #662], http://www.gutenberg.org/cache/epub/662/pg662.txt

195 Wikipedia contributors. Excise [Internet]. Wikipedia, The Free Encyclopedia; 2018 Dec 5, 03:32 UTC [cited 2019 Jan 14]. Available from: https://en.wikipedia.org/w/index.php?title=Excise&oldid=872095128.

196 Micra, Inc., Plainfield, N.J., *1913 Webster's Unabridged Dictionary version 0.50 Letters D and E* (Springfield, Mass.: C. & G. Merriam Co., 1913), Last Edited: February 11, 1999 [E Text #662], http://www.gutenberg.org/cache/epub/662/pg662.txt

197 Wikipedia contributors, "Exculpatory evidence," *Wikipedia, The Free Encyclopedia,* https://en.wikipedia.org/w/index.php?title=Exculpatory_evidence&oldid=875094554 (accessed December 31, 2018).

198 Micra, Inc., Plainfield, N.J., *1913 Webster's Unabridged Dictionary version 0.50 Letters D and E,* (Springfield, Mass.: C. & G. Merriam Co., 1913), Last Edited: February 11, 1999 [E Text #662], http://www.gutenberg.org/cache/epub/662/pg662.txt

199 Ibid.

200 Wikipedia contributors, "Ex parte,"*Wikipedia, The Free Encyclopedia,* https://en.wikipedia.org/w/index.php?title=Ex_parte&oldid=873368872 (accessed December 31, 2018).

201 Micra, Inc., Plainfield, N.J., *1913 Webster's Unabridged Dictionary version 0.50 Letters F, G and H,* (Springfield, Mass.: C. & G. Merriam

Co., 1913), Last Edited: February 11, 1999 [E Text #663],
http://www.gutenberg.org/cache/epub/663/pg663.txt

[202] Wikipedia contributors, "Felony," *Wikipedia, The Free Encyclopedia,* https://en.wikipedia.org/w/index.php?title=Felony&oldid=829480791 (accessed March 30, 2018).

[203] Wikipedia contributors, "Filibuster in the United States Senate,"*Wikipedia, The Free Encyclopedia,* https://en.wikipedia.org/w/index.php?title=Filibuster_in_the_United_States_Senate&oldid=831305641 (accessed April 19, 2018).

[204] Micra, Inc., Plainfield, N.J., *1913 Webster's Unabridged Dictionary version 0.50 Letters F, G and H,* (Springfield, Mass.: C. & G. Merriam Co., 1913), Last Edited: February 11, 1999 [E Text #663], http://www.gutenberg.org/cache/epub/663/pg663.txt

[205] Wikipedia contributors, "Hammurabi," *Wikipedia, The Free Encyclopedia,* https://en.wikipedia.org/w/index.php?title=Hammurabi&oldid=740679207 (accessed October 1, 2016).

[206] Micra, Inc., Plainfield, N.J., *1913 Webster's Unabridged Dictionary version 0.50 Letters F, G and H,* (Springfield, Mass.: C. & G. Merriam Co., 1913), Last Edited: February 11, 1999 [E Text #663], http://www.gutenberg.org/cache/epub/663/pg663.txt

[207] Wikipedia contributors, "Household," *Wikipedia, The Free Encyclopedia,* https://en.wikipedia.org/w/index.php?title=Household&oldid=801936208 (accessed October 13, 2017

[208] Micra, Inc., Plainfield, N.J., *1913 Webster's Unabridged Dictionary version 0.50 Letters I, J, K and L,* (Springfield, Mass.: C. & G. Merriam Co., 1913), Last Edited: February 11, 1999 [E Text #664], http://www.gutenberg.org/cache/epub/664/pg664.txt

[209] Ibid.

[210] Ibid.

[211] Ibid.

[212] Ibid.

[213] Wikipedia contributors, "Incest," *Wikipedia, The Free Encyclopedia,* https://en.wikipedia.org/w/index.php?title=Incest&oldid =910726108 (accessed August 16, 2019).

[214] Micra, Inc., Plainfield, N.J., *1913 Webster's Unabridged Dictionary version 0.50 Letters I, J, K and L,* (Springfield, Mass.: C. & G. Merriam Co., 1913), Last Edited: February 11, 1999 [E Text #664], http://www.gutenberg.org/cache/epub/664/pg664.txt

[215] Ibid.

[216] Ibid.

[217] Ibid.

[218] Ibid.

[219] Wikipedia contributors, "Initiatives and referendums in the United States, "*Wikipedia, The Free Encyclopedia,* https://en.wikipedia.org/w/index.php?title=Initiatives_and_referendum s_in_the_United_States&oldid=850709509 (accessed September 4, 2018).

[220] Micra, Inc., Plainfield, N.J., *1913 Webster's Unabridged Dictionary version 0.50 Letters I, J, K and L,* (Springfield, Mass.: C. & G. Merriam Co., 1913), Last Edited: February 11, 1999 [E Text #664], http://www.gutenberg.org/cache/epub/664/pg664.txt

[221] Wikipedia contributors, "Insider trading, "*Wikipedia, The Free Encyclopedia,* https://en.wikipedia.org/w/index.php?title=Insider_trading&oldid=847439983(accessed August 9, 2018).

[222] Micra, Inc., Plainfield, N.J., *1913 Webster's Unabridged Dictionary version 0.50 Letters I, J, K and L,* (Springfield, Mass.: C. & G. Merriam Co., 1913), Last Edited: February 11, 1999 [E Text #664], http://www.gutenberg.org/cache/epub/664/pg664.txt

[223] Ibid.

[224] Wikipedia contributors, "Judicial review," *Wikipedia, The Free Encyclopedia,* https://en.wikipedia.org/w/index.php?title=Judicial_review&oldid=836876073(accessed May 18, 2018).

[225] Wikipedia contributors, "Jurisdiction," *Wikipedia, The Free Encyclopedia,* https://en.wikipedia.org/w/index.php?title=Jurisdiction&oldid=840143335 (accessed May 17, 2018).

[226] Micra, Inc., Plainfield, N.J., *1913 Webster's Unabridged Dictionary version 0.50 Letters I, J, K and L,* (Springfield, Mass.: C. & G. Merriam Co., 1913), Last Edited: February 11, 1999 [E Text #664], http://www.gutenberg.org/cache/epub/664/pg664.txt

[227] Ibid.

[228] Ibid.

[229] Wikipedia contributors, "Majority," *Wikipedia, The Free Encyclopedia,* https://en.wikipedia.org/w/index.php?title=Majority&oldid=742672277 (accessed October 5, 2016).

230 Wikipedia contributors, "Mandamus," *Wikipedia, The Free Encyclopedia,* https://en.wikipedia.org/w/index.php?title=Mandamus&oldid=866492
https://www.senate.gov/reference/glossary_term/markup.htm664 (accessed November 22, 2018).

231 United States Senate, Glossary Term, Markup, https://www.senate.gov/reference/glossary_term/markup.htm

232 Wikipedia contributors, "Martial law," *Wikipedia, The Free Encyclopedia,* https://en.wikipedia.org/w/index.php?title=Martial_law&oldid=852336953 (accessed September 11, 2018).

233 Wikipedia contributors, "Money laundering," *Wikipedia, The Free Encyclopedia,*
https://en.wikipedia.org/w/index.php?title=Money_laundering&oldid=786716718 (accessed June 23, 2017)

234 Wikipedia contributors, "Nepotism," *Wikipedia, The Free Encyclopedia,* https://en.wikipedia.org/w/index.php?title=Nepotism&oldid=854396463 (accessed August 30, 2018).

235 Wikipedia contributors, "Obstruction of justice," *Wikipedia, The Free Encyclopedia,*
https://en.wikipedia.org/w/index.php?title=Obstruction_of_justice&oldid=786980127 (accessed June 23, 2017)

236 Wikipedia contributors, "Original jurisdiction," *Wikipedia, The Free Encyclopedia,* https://en.wikipedia.org/w/index.php?title=Original_jurisdiction&oldid=838009372(accessed May 17, 2018).

237 Micra, Inc., Plainfield, N.J., *1913 Webster's Unabridged Dictionary version 0.50 Letters P and Q,* (Springfield, Mass.: C. & G. Merriam Co., 1913), Last Edited: February 11, 1999 [E Text #666], http://www.gutenberg.org/cache/epub/666/pg666.txt

[238] Wikipedia contributors, "Party discipline," *Wikipedia, The Free Encyclopedia,* https://en.wikipedia.org/w/index.php?title=Party_discipline&oldid=854519184(accessed September 16, 2018).

[239] Wikipedia contributors, "Perjury," *Wikipedia, The Free Encyclopedia,* https://en.wikipedia.org/w/index.php?title=Perjury&oldid=785901761 (accessed June 23, 2017).

[240] Micra, Inc., Plainfield, N.J., *1913 Webster's Unabridged Dictionary version 0.50 Letters P and Q,* (Springfield, Mass.: C. & G. Merriam Co., 1913), Last Edited: February 11, 1999 [E Text #666], http://www.gutenberg.org/cache/epub/666/pg666.txt

[241] Ibid.

[242] Ibid.

[243] Ibid.

[244] Ibid.

[245] Ibid.

[246]Wikipedia contributors, "Prisoner of war," *Wikipedia, The Free Encyclopedia,* https://en.wikipedia.org/w/index.php?title=Prisoner_of_war&oldid=829202979(accessed March 9, 2018).

[247] Wikipedia contributors, "Probable cause," *Wikipedia, The Free Encyclopedia,* https://en.wikipedia.org/w/index.php?title=Probable_cause&oldid=854496516(accessed August 30, 2018).

[248] Micra, Inc., Plainfield, N.J., *1913 Webster's Unabridged Dictionary version 0.50 Letters P and Q,* (Springfield, Mass.: C. & G. Merriam Co., 1913), Last Edited: February 11, 1999 [E Text #666], http://www.gutenberg.org/cache/epub/666/pg666.txt

[249] Ibid.

[250] Micra, Inc., Plainfield, N.J., *1913 Webster's Unabridged Dictionary version 0.50 Letter R,* (Springfield, Mass.: C. & G. Merriam Co., 1913), Last Edited: February 11, 1999 [E Text #667], http://www.gutenberg.org/cache/epub/667/pg667.txt

[251] Wikipedia contributors, "Referendum," *Wikipedia, The Free Encyclopedia,* https://en.wikipedia.org/w/index.php?title=Referendum&oldid=854734097 (accessed September 4, 2018).

[252] Micra, Inc., Plainfield, N.J., *1913 Webster's Unabridged Dictionary version 0.50 Letter R,* (Springfield, Mass.: C. & G. Merriam Co., 1913), Last Edited: February 11, 1999 [E Text #667], http://www.gutenberg.org/cache/epub/667/pg667.txt

[253] Ibid.

[254] Ibid.

[255] Micra, Inc., Plainfield, N.J., *1913 Webster's Unabridged Dictionary version 0.50 Letter S,* (Springfield, Mass.: C. & G. Merriam Co., 1913), Last Edited: February 11, 1999 [E Text #668], http://www.gutenberg.org/cache/epub/668/pg668.txt

[256] Ibid.

[257] Wikipedia contributors, "Separation of powers," *Wikipedia, The Free*

Encyclopedia, https://en.wikipedia.org/w/index.php?title=Separation_of_powers&oldid=852415515 (accessed August 6, 2018).

[258] Micra, Inc., Plainfield, N.J., *1913 Webster's Unabridged Dictionary version 0.50 Letter S,* (Springfield, Mass.: C. & G. Merriam Co., 1913), Last Edited: February 11, 1999 [E Text #668], http://www.gutenberg.org/cache/epub/668/pg668.txt

[259] Ibid.

[260] Wikipedia contributors, "Sic," *Wikipedia, The Free Encyclopedia,* https://en.wikipedia.org/w/index.php?title=Sic&oldid=827826060 (accessed April 12, 2018).

[261] Micra, Inc., Plainfield, N.J., *1913 Webster's Unabridged Dictionary version 0.50 Letter S,* (Springfield, Mass.: C. & G. Merriam Co., 1913), Last Edited: February 11, 1999 [E Text #668], http://www.gutenberg.org/cache/epub/668/pg668.txt

[262] Wikipedia contributors, "Snap election," *Wikipedia, The Free Encyclopedia,* https://en.wikipedia.org/w/index.php?title=Snap_election&oldid=846907511 (accessed September 5, 2018).

[263] Micra, Inc., Plainfield, N.J., *1913 Webster's Unabridged Dictionary version 0.50 Letter S,* (Springfield, Mass.: C. & G. Merriam Co., 1913), Last Edited: February 11, 1999 [E Text #668], http://www.gutenberg.org/cache/epub/668/pg668.txt

[264] Ibid.

[265] Wikipedia contributors, "Precedent," *Wikipedia, The Free Encyclopedia,* https://en.wikipedia.org/w/index.php?title=Precedent&oldid=880709008 (accessed February 9, 2019).

[266] Micra, Inc., Plainfield, N.J., *1913 Webster's Unabridged Dictionary version 0.50 Letter S,* (Springfield, Mass.: C. & G. Merriam Co.,

1913), Last Edited: February 11, 1999 [E Text #668], http://www.gutenberg.org/cache/epub/668/pg668.txt

[267] Ibid.

[268] Ibid.

[269] Ibid.

[270] Wikipedia contributors, "Supreme court," *Wikipedia, The Free Encyclopedia,* https://en.wikipedia.org/w/index.php?title=Supreme_court&oldid=847824085(accessed August 23, 2018).

[271] Wikipedia contributors, "Tariff," *Wikipedia, The Free Encyclopedia,* https://en.wikipedia.org/w/index.php?title=Tariff&oldid=835919908 (accessed April 12, 2018).

[272] Micra, Inc., Plainfield, N.J., *1913 Webster's Unabridged Dictionary version 0.50 Letters T,U,V and W,* (Springfield, Mass.: C. & G. Merriam Co., 1913), Last Edited: February 11, 1999 [E Text #669], http://www.gutenberg.org/cache/epub/669/pg669.txt

[273] Wikipedia contributors, "Tort," *Wikipedia, The Free Encyclopedia,* Wikipedia contributors https://en.wikipedia.org/w/index.php?title=Tort&oldid=867858196 (accessed November 9, 2018).

[274] Micra, Inc., Plainfield, N.J., *1913 Webster's Unabridged Dictionary version 0.50 Letters T,U,V and W,* (Springfield, Mass.: C. & G. Merriam Co., 1913), Last Edited: February 11, 1999 [E Text #669], http://www.gutenberg.org/cache/epub/669/pg669.txt

[275] Ibid.

[276] Wikipedia contributors, "Pensions crisis," *Wikipedia, The Free Encyclopedia,* https://en.wikipedia.org/w/index.php?title=Pensions_crisis&oldid=854866912(accessed September 10, 2018).

[277] Micra, Inc., Plainfield, N.J., *1913 Webster's Unabridged Dictionary version 0.50 Letters T,U,V and W,* (Springfield, Mass.: C. & G. Merriam Co., 1913), Last Edited: February 11, 1999 [E Text #669],

[278] Wikipedia contributors, "Victimless crime," *Wikipedia, The Free Encyclopedia,* https://en.wikipedia.org/w/index.php?title=Victimless_crime&oldid=830733187(accessed April 3, 2018).

[279] Micra, Inc., Plainfield, N.J., *1913 Webster's Unabridged Dictionary version 0.50 Letters T,U,V and W,* (Springfield, Mass.: C. & G. Merriam Co., 1913), Last Edited: February 11, 1999 [E Text #669], http://www.gutenberg.org/cache/epub/669/pg669.txt

[280] Wikipedia contributors, "Warrant (law)," *Wikipedia, The Free Encyclopedia,* https://en.wikipedia.org/w/index.php?title=Warrant_(law)&oldid=861024097 (accessed December 11, 2018).

[281] Wikipedia contributors, "Witness tampering," *Wikipedia, The Free Encyclopedia,* https://en.wikipedia.org/w/index.php?title=Witness_tampering&oldid=871853475(accessed December 11, 2018).

[282] Wikipedia contributors, "Writ," *Wikipedia, The Free Encyclopedia,* https://en.wikipedia.org/w/index.php?title=Writ&oldid=867460671 (accessed November 10, 2018).

181

The woods are lovely, dark and deep,
But I have promises to keep,
And miles to go before I sleep,
And miles to go before I sleep.
                              Robert Frost

183

Thanks for reading me.

ABOUT THE AUTHOR

Rohit (Roy) Kajaria

The author is an Electrical Engineer with a Bachelor of Technology degree from the Indian Institute of Technology Bombay, Mumbai, India and a Master of Science degree from the Montana State University, Bozeman, Montana, USA. He served honorably in the U.S. Army from 1971 through 1974, and became a U.S. citizen in 1973. He lives with his wife and daughter in Oakton, Virginia.